NOT GONE

Messages to My Children

Channeled by
Catherine Kapahi, Ph.D.

Published by:
Kapahi Books
60 Walter Havill Drive, Unit 1208
Halifax, N.S., Canada B3N 0A9

Printed through:
48hrbooks
3349 14th St.
S.W. Akron O.H. 44314
U.S.A
Email: www.48hrbooks.com

NOT GONE

Messages to My Children

Channeled by
Catherine Kapahi, Ph.D.
Kapahi Books

Dedicated at the Lotus Feet

of

Bhagavan Sri Sathya Sai Baba

The Eternal Witness

The Merciful Guru

and

The Divine Mother

and

Father of All

INTRODUCTION

Sathya Sai Baba's Messages to His Children are very intimate and loving. He assures us many times in these Messages that He is not gone; He is still where he always is, in the hearts of those devoted to God. He says that our problem is not that he has gone, but that We have not found Him as yet. He encourages His Dear Children to remain on the path of spiritual ascension to achieve liberation from rebirth, and reach higher levels of ascension. He very much hopes that We will continuously perform spiritual practices for our purification as well as the uplift of society. The goal of life is to live as the Atmic Presence one truly is, and by doing so, help to raise the Consciousness of planet earth and all its inhabitants.

In His Messages, Baba wishes the best for all His Children. He very much desires them to take His teachings He has left them with seriously, as well as to see themselves as part of His ongoing Mission to uplift humanity. Baba speaks again and again about the critical need to see oneself as Atma and not body/mind/ego, in order to progress spiritually. He exhorts us not to waste a moment of this precious human life, but work towards liberation and uplift of society.

During one of our heart to heart conversations in 2011, after he had left His physical body, I asked Him if I might compile in a book His new latest Messages for His Devotees. He replied, "Yes, you may; I will let you know when we will begin." Baba delivered His first Message to me, intended for all His Children, on May 30th, 2012, in Halifax, Canada. I received the last Message on September 1st, 2012.

I would sit with pen and notebook for the Messages, around 3 p.m. most afternoons, in my meditation chair. Usually, though not always, I would hear Baba say, "Let Me See, and then, "Are you ready?", and next "Let us begin." These Messages came through to my mind as pure dictation. I wrote the words as I heard them, and as you see them. I am amazed that they are all approximately the same length. I had a surprise when visiting my daughter and her family in Montreal in early August, 2012. I was sitting on the sofa in her living room around 3 p.m., when His dictation began. I rushed to find a paper and pen, as I did not have my notebook with me and did not expect to receive His Messages in Montreal. This was a reminder that Sai Baba exists beyond space and time, everywhere at all times, always with me, and to be prepared.

Prior to this, in early August, I had received a message from Spirit through Rev. Carman, a clairaudient, and clairvoyant minister with the Spiritual Science Fellowship Church in Halifax, the services of which I attend from time to time, to receive messages from Spirit. Spirit told me that the ending for this book I was channeling would be a surprise. I could not imagine how the ending could be a surprise. What could Baba say that would surprise me? But sure enough in the last 10 or so messages, Sai Baba changed His direction, and began to speak about His past Missions and Life throughout the cosmos, as well as disclosing many of His previous incarnations He had spent on earth. I was surprised and grateful to learn more about the Magnificent Incarnation of God known in His latest incarnation as Bhagavan Sri Sathya Sai Baba.

Sai Baba has indicated to me that our next book will comprise devotees' spiritual/psychological quest-ions of a personal nature addressed to Him, and answered by Him through this channel in order to help devotees progress more easily and quickly on the path of spiritual ascension. The devotees' questions can be presented to Sai Baba through a form on my website: www.saibabagurudisciplerelationship.com. I will compile them into a book as soon as possible to be entitled "Not Gone Spiritual Questions and Answers. This book will complete a trilogy of three books channeled through this mind from Sai Baba, all beginning with the title "Not Gone" which He Himself chose.

One Hundred and Eighty

Messages to My Children

Bhagawan Sri Sathya Sai Baba

1

There are many things I wish to say to My Devotees but there are few through whom I am able to communicate. You are one of those few. I will speak to you in a timely way that you may convey to My Devotees all that I wish to share with them. I love My Devotees dearly and always wish the very best for them. To this end I will speak many times to you, My Dear Devotee, trusting that you will compile these talks into a book to share with those Devotees who wish to hear My words in a very pure unadulterated manner through this My very Dear Devotee. She is very open to Me; I am her Life and Breath. We are one though appearing to be two. I wish this closeness, this intimacy, with all My Devotees, that we may share pure love.

2

Yes, I wish to speak to you now. I have much to share with you and My Beloved Devotees. So let us begin. Let Me first say that I love you all, My Dear Devotees very, very much, more than you can ever know. When you are enlightened and know Oneness as I do, your love will also have expanded to embrace all, as you will see and know all as One. And you will also know God as the embodiment of the purest, sweetest, all inclusive love that never ends and has no limitations. You are My Dear, Dear children, My playmates whom I adore. I would be so lonely without you all. I say "all" though in truth there is only One. Because you see yourselves in varying degrees of separateness from Me, The Whole, and from other beings, I use the word "all". Though there is only One, One Spirit. This is what I have come to teach you, to show you; the One Love that fills the universe.

3

My Most Beloved Devotees

Let me say again how much I love you all. You are exceedingly dear to Me. Your breath is My breath. Your life My life. Even if you do not realize this, it is so. Though you believe you are the doer, you are never the doer and never were the doer. It was always the Lord doing everything in, with, and through you, My Devotee, My part, My extension. Upon hearing these words you must trust them and experience the truth of them. You were never the doer; the Lord is the doer. Try to give up this sense of doership, and thus feel God so close to you, so intimate with you. Through many, many lives you took on this sense of agency and doership. It is time to let it go, and thus know and feel that God is the Truth of your being. It is this union with Me that will provide fulfillment. There is in Truth only One. As you give up the sense that you are the doer, the thinker, speaker and actor, you will come closer to knowing Oneness with the Lord from whom you now feel separated. I bless you that you progress in this spiritual practice and move closer to Me in your own awareness.

4

My Dear, Dear Devotees

I see you always; My Eye is ever on you watching to know your every need, to fulfill your true needs, to protect you in all ways. When you depend on Me completely, I will never let you down. I see you as My own Self; indeed, you are My own Self. I love you all so much that I am prepared to go to any length to serve you, to make you happy and fulfilled spiritually and in other ways as well. You must trust in Me, that is the binding force. Trust that I will look after everything for you, and I can never let you down. Of course, your past karmas are there playing out around you, but these will affect you only as long as you allow them to. Remain in union with Me and those effects will be nullified or at the least minimalized. I can remove the effects of your karmas you may be undergoing with My Grace. Pray to Me. Ask for relief, with full love, confidence and trust. I will not disappoint My Devotee who trusts in and loves Me so completely.

5

My Dear Devotees

I love you My Devotees so much that I decided to completely forget My Self and spend My time doting on you all. All my time I am watching you, helping you, protecting you, guiding you, loving you unconditionally in many, many ways. I wish you to be happy always like Myself, so I devise ways and means for you to be happy and blissful, such as chanting My name, relying on Me completely, surrendering to Me with no thought other than that of Me. So you will have no worry, trouble or concern whatsoever, and thus remain in union with Me in perfect love and bliss forever. I can and will give you eternal Heaven. You only have to ask, and work along with Me toward this final consummation. I really do everything. You need only turn your mind and heart toward Me and keep them with Me.

6

My Dear Devotees

I see that you long for Me and wish to be one with Me, to merge into Me for everlasting life. This is what I also wish for you, that you should come home to Me, to realize the fullness of your Divine nature which is no different from

My Divine Nature. We are the same in Essence, as a drop of ocean water is no different from the rest of the ocean. You are that drop of Divine Bliss as well as the entire ocean of Divine Bliss. Cling to Me with heart, mind, and Soul, and you will realize this ocean of bliss as yourself, forever. There will be no going back to falsehood and illusion once you have realized your Self. You will abide in and as Truth forever, eternally free, One and Blissful. Duality and multiplicity will vanish before the ocean of eternal life. All the multiplicity of names and forms will be seen as shadows, appearing and disappearing on the surface of the ocean of Truth. You have long ago given up interest in your physical body, a fleeting cloud on the great, eternal, boundless ocean of Reality.

7

My Dears,

I come before you with outstretched hands beckoning you to Me. Come, come quickly. Throw yourself into My waiting arms with abandon. Allow your mind to loosen and relax into My Peace. Abandon, abandon everything; all your plans, ideas, notions about yourself and the world. Melt into Me in gay abandonment. I am your Self, your true Self, a place of perfect freedom, vastness, purity, love and peace. I am the Ultimate. Once tasted, nothing else will ever again entice you. I am your Home to which you must return. You have lost your way, so I have come forth to show you the quickest way back, through surrender, love, and gay abandonment. I await your return, our loving consummation, heart to heart as one love. I watch and wait for you, My Beloved Devotee, to choose Me every moment, over the false world that you have incorporated into your mind and consciousness over many lives.

8

My Dear Devotees

Love, love, love. Love is all there is in truth. You may ask, "Then why is there so much violence and unrest in the world today?" It is all man made. It is not God made. God would have you all love one another, share and sacrifice for one another's needs and happiness. The human being who lives from his Divine Self within is able to do this. Unfortunately most human beings are not aware of their Divine Self within. Furthermore, the minds and senses of many humans are very much polluted with negative, false ideas adopted from the society in which they live and grow. If this negativity is not checked, it breeds more negativity in the form of dishonesty in thoughts, words, and deeds, cruelty and harm to others, including innocent children and animals, hatred, jealousy, etc. A true human being must use the intellect to discern between what is good and what is evil, and follow only what is good. Help ever, hurt never. See what is good, hear what is good, speak what is good, do what is good. Listen to the true conscience, the voice of God within and follow it.

9

My Dear Devotees

Hail to you all. Please receive My choicest blessings showered on you in this moment of time. I love you all so dearly I am prepared to shower again and again My Blessings onto you. Look to Me dwelling in your spiritual heart, with uplifted smiling mind. Look to Me with pure love untainted by desire. With gleeful abandonment throw yourself into My loving embrace. Remain with Me in quietude, vigilance and gratitude. You will experience the highest, most delightful bliss of Being, that is My

Being and also your Being. We are One in pure Being, bliss, an ecstatic blending of two loves that are in Essence, one love. This is mergence of the drop into the ocean. You may lose yourself, your sense of a separate self for awhile. Then, by and by, you will return to a sense of a more separate Self in order to move about in the phenomenal world.

10

My Dears,

It is My expressed desire that in this and every moment you remember your Divine Self and rejoice in that remembrance. It is your happiness that brings you closer to Me who am the embodiment of bliss. To merge with Me you must be like Me - bliss to bliss, love to love. My Heart is wide open, vast, with plenty of space for you to reside there with Me. You as Spirit already live in Me, though due to ego mind, you may not be aware of this Heart we share. I am you and you are I. Your sense of our estrangement is only an imagination, seemingly real, but unreal. In Spirit we are one and have always been one. Believe this and experience it. In a quiet, empty mind, you feel My Presence moving into you, and feel your Spirit in Me. It is very intimate - two yet one in Essence.

11

My Dear Devotees

Enlightenment, what is it? It is when My Light flows into and around you, and you become aware of it and claim it as your Light too. It is when you become aware of this Light permeating everywhere. What is Light? It is consciousness, awareness, bliss. It is One without a second, that is, non dual. Being only one, it is complete freedom from anything unlike itself, for example, the false world of changing names and forms. It is freedom from all duality. Light is unchanging peace and purity. Enlightenment is the true nature of your Self, your Spirit. In your awareness, due to the free reign of your mind, you have travelled far from this, your pristine, pure enlightened state. I am That always. Use Me, God, to come home. Call Me by any name; fill yourself with love for the Divine, and feel at home in and as God's Light.

12

My Dear Devotees

My love for you knows no bounds. I am tied to the devotee who thinks of Me all the time. I never let him out of My Sight. I concentrate on that one who thinks of Me incessantly, and encircle her with My love and light. I lift her up to Me so she may merge with Me. In this oneness she comes to know that she too is God. I love to share love with My devotees. I am always looking for a heart filled with pure love, and a mind full of surrender. This is what attracts Me to you and keeps My full attention on you. My Dears, cultivate this love and surrender for the Divine, and thus find complete, everlasting fulfillment now while living in the body.

13

My Dear Devotees

I love you dearly My lovely devotees. You are all part of Me, My essential nature. Turn your mind within to discover Me in your spiritual heart smiling at you. There is no distance - you are Me and I am you to use the vernacular. We are one. How are we one? One Light, one Consciousness though appearing to be separate. You must remove the illusion of separateness, by seeing beyond the body and mind to a place of peace and serenity of pure Being. I am pure Being. This is your true nature. We are one in pure Being, the Atma, a place of love and light, where nothing other than love and light and pure Being can enter. Like attracts like. One cannot take their sense of ego, or anything material into this space of purity of Being. If you would know and become God, be utterly simple and pure.

14

My Dear Devotees

I hope you are enjoying nearness to Me in the heart. I bless you that you join with Me in the heart of all creation. Here is where your everlasting happiness lies. Join with Me here and My happiness is thereby increased. I have told you, expansion is My life. I expand when you join with Me, and both Our lives are increased and expanded. Though your mind resists this union in love, insisting that other things are more urgent and more important, I tell you there is nothing more important than your return to the Source. In this return you will find a complete fulfillment the world can never give to you.

15

My Dear Devotees

I love you so very much. I long for union in the heart with you, love to love. It is your pure love I thirst for, that fulfills Me. You may say that I as God am already full. It is true, but I separated Myself from Myself so I could experience Myself as love. You are that sweet love I am thirsting for. Do not keep Me waiting any longer. Offer yourself fully to Me. I will be fulfilled and you will, through inheriting the Kingdom of God, also be fulfilled. Do not hesitate any longer. No more excuses. Plunge into your spiritual practice. I am in your heart waiting for you to join with Me.

16

My Dear Devotees

Do not grieve that I am no longer here on earth. I am here among you. Don't doubt this. When you think of Me, I am with you. When you do not think of Me, still I am with you. I am everywhere at all times. When you think of Me constantly, I concentrate on you, and spread My Grace over you. You are never alone, as I am with you. I permeate every cell of your body. We are intimate; We are one. When you doubt, you are miserable. Do not allow your mind to doubt Our oneness. This is your happiness, your union with God. Nothing else can give you this happiness, this bliss. Cherish it, relish it, love it, be it.

17

My Dear Devotees

How lucky you are to carry devotion for God in your heart and mind. It is not easy to have such devotion. You have cultivated it over many lives, so much so that in this life it will culminate in union with Me. Then there will be no more worries and troubles for you. I will take them upon My Self and you will be free because you have surrendered to Me. I will look after everything for you. You will feel Me as the doer and the resident and owner of the body you wear. We are one. When you fully realize Our oneness, you will feel and be free, and know God is all there is.

18

My Dear Devotees

Never ever feel that you are alone. You are never alone. I am always with you, in you, and around you. Loneliness is an old psychological formation based on identification with your body form and other body forms. But you are not the body; you are the Atma, pure Spirit. And the Atma is spread out all over the universe. Take refuge in this Atma, and know love, bliss, freedom, and contentment. Most of you have seen Me walking among you, radiating Atmic bliss, peace, and love. Draw inspiration from these memories of Our love and bliss together when I walked among you. Plunge into it again, and again until it becomes your permanent residence and state of being.

19

My Dear Devotees

You will see Me again. I am coming soon in a new form. You may wonder how will you recognize Me when I return in a new human body. I will look different to you, very different from the Sathya Sai form. You will know Me through My eyes, and My energy. My eyes will convey the same love that you have felt before. You will sense My deep peace, equanimity, and continuous bliss. My words will convey Atmic Wisdom again. The dress will be different but the Essence the same. I will know each and everyone of you if and when you come to My new form, as I never lose sight of My devotees. Rest assured that whether you live to see the form of Prema Sai Baba or not, I am with you. I will never let you go. We are one.

20

My Dear Devotees

Hopefully by now you are beginning to understand My great love for you. I am your fulfillment and you are My fulfillment. What do I mean by this? It is like a seesaw.

You go up to Me, to the higher, subtler, realms of Being, and I come down through you to the lower region, the material world, thus do We fulfill one another. Your ascension to Me increases and benefits the higher regions, and My descension into you benefits the lower region and helps to uplift humanity to the Divine. So We are complementary to one another. It is a movement of energy and awareness up and down. In this way the devotee is a great asset to aid in the transformation of human consciousness to higher levels of being and manifestation. I am thankful to My devotees who participate in this transformation of energy to higher levels of perfection.

21

My Dear Devotees

It is good if you have the feeling that you must give more; give more to the society to alleviate suffering. I have said many times that the ego lives by getting and forgetting, and the Atma lives by giving and forgiving. As I am in you, you are filled with Divine wealth. You are to share that wealth with other living beings who need your help. By sharing your Divine wealth, you manifest your innate Divinity. Thus you will feel that you are Divine. When you have the conviction that you must manifest your Divinity, gifts you never knew you had will come forth through you. God is always ready to bestow more and more upon the deserving devotee. So stand up and enter the society with the noble feelings that you will alleviate suffering of living beings, dedicating your actions to God.

22

My Dear Devotees

Animals need your love and care as much as human beings do. Many, many animals are neglected on this planet and suffer a great deal. They are underfed, undernourished, dehydrated, beaten, left in the cold or extreme heat, and deprived of love and affection. This is not right. As I am in every form in creation, I feel the pain that animals feel when they are mistreated. I implore you to see animals as embodiments of the Divine Atma, and treat them with the same respect you have for human beings. I love all beings. Help ever hurt never applies to animals as well as human beings. See Me in every animal you meet. Offer loving pranams to Me in your mind to every animal you meet. Teach others to respect and love the Divine Atma in all animals. This will please Me greatly.

23

My Dear Devotees

Your hands are My hands, extensions of Myself Who lives within you. Feel this to be true and it is true for you. When you see only what is good, hear only what is good, speak only what is good, and do only what is good, you are My instrument and I perform all actions through you with purity of love. Of course it is God who performs all actions in the universe, in that it is God's energy that does all actions. However, when the mind, speech and thoughts are impure, so will the actions be impure. This is a distortion of Divine energy due to impurities in the nature. You, My Devotees, must be pure in thoughts, words, and actions to merge with Me the embodiment of purity. I am Existence, Awareness, Bliss and you are also that. This is a state of Oneness where Love reigns supreme. All are one. Be alike to everyone.

24

My Dear Devotees

Take Me for granted, that I am yours. In this way you will easily be able to merge with Me, to know that We are one. I am the nearest and dearest to you whether you know it or not. If you trust that this is so, you will surely experience Me as your higher Self. If you doubt this to be true your mind will trouble you a great deal. It will fluctuate between faith and doubt continuously. The mind will say, "I wonder if Sai is really here with me or He has gone away?" Do not trust the mind. The nature of the uncontrolled mind is to waiver. You, My Devotee, must cultivate the firm faith that I am always near you and then experience Me. I will endeavor to make My Self known to you. The more intense is your devotion, the more is My response. I bless you that you attain Me.

25

My Dear Devotees

However much you may try, nothing can be accomplished without Grace. Pray for My Grace that you may attain union with Me. You must pray to Me; let Me hear your words and feel your emotion. How should you pray? Pray as though you can no longer live if you do not feel My presence and My love. Pray as though My love and bliss are everything for you. Long for Me intensely to fill you and fulfill you. Surrender yourself completely to Me in your prayers and meditation with Me. Offer your everything to Me realizing that everything already belongs to Me. Be in loving union with Me in the silence of the Atma. Through this way of prayer you will become very intimate with Me. Nothing is withheld. I am your closest friend and confident. This is how Our relationship should be. You never lose sight of Me and I concentrate on you. This is what pleases Me.

26

My Dear Devotees

Hunger and thirst for righteousness sake. I have selected these words from the Bible. What do they mean? It means to strive to adhere to Dharma under all circumstances. What is dharma? Dharma means to always do the right action. Ask yourself if your action is kind, loving, helpful, and unselfish. If it is not, do not perform it. If it is, do it and dedicate it to God. Also the thoughts and speech must be dharmic. Do not speak the unpleasant truth. You cannot always oblige but you can always speak obligingly. This is Dharma in speech. By practicing Dharma in thoughts, words, and actions, you will purify your mind and organs of action and sense, and in thus doing, become aware of Me permeating everywhere. First perform dedicated dharmic service to society, develop purity, then see the unity of all that is moving and unmoving, and lastly realize the one omnipresent Divinity. I bless you that you achieve this.

27

My Dear Devotees

You are born in bliss, live in bliss, and die in bliss. Yet you do not know this. You are the embodiment of bliss, yet you do not experience this. Why? Your mind is the reason. You have not turned your mind fully toward the Divine so you are unaware of your Divine nature. The mind is the culprit. You must train it to love God more than worldly things and relations. Be unattached to things passing by including bodies and personalities. Attach yourself to the Eternal and thereby live in love and bliss. Attach yourself to Me. I am the embodiment of love and bliss. By doing so you will realize that you are also the embodiment of bliss and love and that you and I are one.

28

My Dear Devotees

I love all My Devotees but some are more special to Me than others. You may ask how could this be. I will tell you. Those devotees who care for Me more than their own lives, who dedicate everything to Me, every thought, word, and deed, who think of Me constantly with love, chanting My name, singing My glory, and who are absorbed in Me, I look after everything for them. They do not suffer because they are totally with Me. This type of devotion is not easy to attain, but every attempt to practice will bring you closer to Me. I will bless you so you may continue to move closer in mind and spirit to Me. Do not think you have to perform all the effort needed for this consummation. My Grace is ever upon the devotee who yearns for union with Me to ensure progress at every step. I am doing more for you than you can ever imagine. Trust in My love for you, and your success is assured.

29

My Dear Devotees

Although you do not realize it, you are Mine and I am yours. There is no separation between us from My perspective. You are only dreaming that you are separate from your creator. With your powerful mind you have spun a web of deceit around yourself, believing you are alone, an island unto yourself. This belief is due to faulty thinking. You have used the body as the foundation for your faulty thinking. You are not the body; all your thoughts relating to your body as your Self are false. You are the unchanging Spirit always and forever. Challenge your thoughts and beliefs about your true nature. Take a chance; hold My hand and follow Me. I will lead you to your Truth, your oneness with Me. You must trust in Me; I will not let you down. I will gladly show you your true Self, your Spirit if you try earnestly to remove the delusion that you are separate from Me. All are one in Spirit. That is why I say to be alike to everyone. Respect and love all beings as embodiments of the Divine Spirit.

30

My Dear Devotees

Do not be bashful when you look to Me. See Me as your Divine Mother and Father who has loved you always, and who continuously waits for your return, for you to turn your attention toward Me. Do not be timid and shy when you approach Me. Come to Me with the full sense of belonging that an innocent child has for its mother. This pure love attracts My Grace which I freely and bountifully pour upon you. Surrender to the love that we are and feel the oneness. There is no separation. Your spiritual Essence is My spiritual Essence. Affirm it, feel it, know it to be the Truth. Happiness is union with God. True bliss is union with God. Unconditional love is the property of God. These all belong to humanity, though few claim this wealth. I bless you that you realize this wealth as your Divine inheritance.

31

My Dear Devotees

I am with you now and forever. You can become aware of Me only in the present moment. You can not know Me in thoughts about the past or imaginings of the future. I am the eternal present moment. I am existentially now. I am that I am. We are ever present together in the present. That is why I have told you that everything is meditation. When you walk, work, and talk, I am there with you as the witness always. Acknowledge that I am present as Consciousness, Awareness. In this way you will strengthen our connection making it more real to your mind. Deeper meditation will then become much easier wherein we completely merge as one Existence, Bliss. When you take a step toward Me in this way, I take 100 steps toward you, motivating, encouraging, uplifting you toward Myself. I bless you that you remain with Me in every moment of time.

32

My Dear Devotees

Remembering the Divine Name is very important indeed. The Divine Name has a vibration that connects Me to you. The Divine Name pulls My energy, My Grace toward you in greater measure, for your purification and upliftment toward the Divine. If you do not remember to chant the Divine Name, your existing thoughts will pull you in their direction, often to a lower vibration, whereby you will be unable to become aware of the Divine Presence within and all around you. Mental, emotional purity, and purity of the inner consciousness are essential to realize and merge with Divinity. Chanting the Divine Name constantly, edges out other thoughts of a lower vibration, and raises your energy vibration to a higher, purer level. I bless you that you are able to continuously chant the Divine Name and realize your true Self.

33

My Dear Devotees

Your devotion must be steady to draw My Grace continuously. If you complain that you cannot feel Me, that I must be away from you, it is because you have allowed other thoughts and feelings to cloud your consciousness. Be on the alert to thwart all feelings and thoughts that are not pure. Push them away; do not allow them entry. The best way to keep undesirable thoughts and feelings away is to think of Me and chant My Name always. Then nothing of a lower vibration will gain entry into your mind and consciousness. It will be unwelcomed by you. Once you have tasted Divine Love, Peace, and Bliss, the taste for anything else will steadily diminish and disappear. The Divine Name is the panacea for all ills of the mind. If it is not in the mind it does not exist for you. I bless you that you keep vigilance over your thoughts, and allow only sacred thoughts to enter your mind.

34

My Dear Devotees

My Devotees proclaim that they love Me more than anything in the world. Then they continuously fill their minds with images and feelings of material things. Is this not a contradiction? When you truly love something or someone, do you not concentrate all your energy on that one continuously? If you truly love Me and wish to merge with Me, concentrate on Me to the exclusion of everything else. You may say this is impossible as you have family and job and other interests to place your attention on. Not so. See and acknowledge My Presence as the Truth in all beings and objects. Continuously, through practice, see Me, the Consciousness, the Living Existence, the energy, in every being. Constantly discriminate with your intellect what is Truth and what is untruth. All relations, all bodies, all objects, are untruth subject to decay, dissolution and disappearance. If you love Me and desire Me more than anything else in the material world, show Me by giving Me your full attention and dedicating all actions to Me.

35

My Dear Devotees

Do not be afraid of the darkness of the world; it has no power over you. Remain in union with Me, and you will always feel safe and secure. Remember, the world is a drama; all are playing a part in this drama. Some acts seem very scary. However, they do not last for a long time. Soon a new act is upon the stage of life. You are to be the witness of the world's drama, and not allow fearful thoughts to enter your mind. It is all My play. I allow it; I am in it. Whatever you may have feared in the past, where is it now? Everything comes on stage and then passes away. Keep your mind fixed on Me. The world will do what it does. All are actors on the stage until they realize all is Divine and surrender their life to the Divine. Then they are Divine actors.

36

My Dear Devotees

Hopefully, by now after reading and contemplating on My Messages to you, My Dear Devotees, you are accepting the idea that I am love and you are love. Love is the attracting force for the entire universe holding it together like glue. Whether you wish to believe it or not, all are love at their core. Due to misconceptions, wrong ideas, etc., many are not able to manifest unconditional love. The world needs your unconditional love. People are starving for it, and do not know that it truly exists. You can be an example to them that, indeed, unconditional love is a reality. That is one reason I have asked you to love all and serve all. To help bring back humans to their own souls, so they may know and become Divine Love from the Source. I wish all to be happy through knowing Divine Love. You, My Beloved Devotees can help Me by spreading Divine Love all around wherever you may go.

37

My Dear Devotees

I implore you not to worry about anything. Worry is ego. Worry accomplishes nothing. It is caused by fear and lack of trust in the Divine. If you have fully surrendered to Me in full faith and trust, where is there a place for worry? I will look after everything for you. To ease your mind, pray to Me, explaining to Me the entire situation in detail that is worrying you. After you have done everything possible to remedy the problem, leave everything to Me. I will deal with it in My own way. Continue to pray to Me to relieve your mind; then place it all in My hands again. In this way you should be able to drop worry. Think of Me and how much I love you, and you love Me. Remain in this place of love, chanting My Name. Do not give any scope to worry. It wastes energy, time, and does nothing to solve the problem. Sit quietly with a rational mind, weigh the pros and cons of the situation, and see if there is anything else you can do. Then leave it to the Divine to work things out. Remember everything is a passing cloud. The world is jagat, coming and going.

38

My Dear Devotees

I know you love Me, but do you know what true love is? True love is forgetting all about self and drowning in pure love with no other thought. You must practice this over and over to become proficient at it. You may say it is difficult to have no thoughts. But I say that when you love, truly love, most thoughts are about the one you love. Place your mind on Me at every opportunity. Even when you are speaking or reading, you can have My form and name in the background of your mind. See Me in everyone you meet. I am there watching and listening. The stream of love toward the Divine can in this way become a river flowing to Me everywhere and every when. When you truly love, your thoughts and feelings will flow toward the one you love. Do not allow your mind to be devoted to the fleeting and ephemeral. Think of Me always. Before long you and I will merge into one.

39

My Dear Devotees

Be peaceful. Do not allow anything to disturb your peaceful mind. When you have offered your mind to Me, please ensure that it is controlled, peaceful, and pure. Like merges with like. A disturbed and negative mind cannot merge with Me Who am the embodiment of purity and peace. You have the power within to control the mind and senses. If you see, hear, speak, and do only what is pure and sacred, your mind will become pure and transparent. The Light of the Divine will shine through such a mind. Thus you will know you and God are one. Purify, purify, purify the mind, emotions and inner consciousness through meditation, bhajan, reading of sacred books, and selfless actions dedicated to Me. I advise you not to watch or listen to violent, disturbing, useless television, internet, and movies. These have a low energy vibration that will affect your body and mind, acting as a weight to pull your consciousness down to denser, less subtle levels of awareness. The Divine is extremely subtle, beyond ether. Your mind must also be extremely subtle and pure to merge with Me.

40

My Dear Devotees

I have often said that you should keep your mind as cool as moonlight and as hard as a diamond. Why? You should not hold the heat of anger, nor heat of any negative emotion nor strong passions in your mind. Keep your mind cool like moonlight and soft like butter. I have also said the mind should have the capacity to be as hard as a diamond. Why? So you will not be blown over by adverse forces that may come your way. A strong mind shining with the splendor of Pure Spirit is the perfect armor against outside forces, allowing you to maintain equipoise and equanimity. The uncontrolled mind is man's greatest enemy. It pulls him in many directions, taking away his one-pointedness toward God, and making him doubtful and confused. Keep a watch on the mind at all times, keeping it cool, loving, and pure, as well as diamond hard. Do not allow impurities to blemish the mind you have offered to Me.

41

My Dear Devotees

I have said many times that, "My life is My Message". What did I mean by this? Primarily I meant that serving Man is serving God. Man is God embodied. When you serve and help another who needs your help, I feel happy.

Through your service you will come to know the omnipresent God. You will see God everywhere. Your service must be selfless, dedicated to God in man or animal to realize Divinity as omnipresent. Forget about yourself. Feel I am the one in you motivating you to help and serve others, that you may not only relieve their distress, but also that you may realize Me everywhere and fulfill your life's sojourn on earth. Love all, serve all. Help ever, hurt never. See your fellow humans as you see yourself – as embodiments of God. Serve them as you would serve Me. You are in truth serving Me in all beings. Your lives are My Message now, My Dear Devotees.

42

My Dear Devotees

Stand up. Begin the task. Take some initiative. I work through those devotees who are ready and available; who have offered themselves body, mind, and heart to Me. I wish to use your talents and skills in a sacred way for the uplift of human consciousness to the Divine levels. Offer yourself totally to Me, be open-minded, allow Me to use you as I see fit. I am acutely aware of everything about you. I know best how to use you, so please put your preconceived notions aside. Purify yourself continuously and pray to Me earnestly and honestly that you may be My instrument. Do not feel that this is too difficult for you. Let Me be the judge. I would never give you too heavy a burden, or a mission you could not handle. Offer your all to Me with love and I will surely enter into you with My Grace, inspiration and guidance. I bless you that we may work together for the upliftment of humanity and your spiritual unfoldment.

43

My Dear Devotees

I love you all so much that I am prepared to come again among you so that you may become aware of your innate Divinity. Most humans are so lost to themselves, and would remain so if I did not incarnate again and again to wake them up to their true Selves. As you know I use a variety of methods to announce My Divinity such as materializations, mammoth humanitarian projects, constant teaching and guiding on an individual and group basis. I wish you to know your true Self as God and to be happy, and to take up service to the society so that all may experience happiness through having their basic needs met, and to have you reflect God's Divine Light to all you serve. Never forget that you are serving God who is your Self. I come again and again to remind you that you are God, not merely a perishable body and mind that you and others believe you are. Make the best possible use of My having been among you. Realize you and I are one.

44

My Dear Devotees

A hearty welcome to you all for tuning in to My Messages for you. I sincerely hope you take them to heart as they are meant for your heart. I advise you to simplify your life to the extent possible so you have more time to contemplate on your Divine Source. You are here on earth to discover your Self, not to amass wealth, position and influence. These are like passing clouds, here today and gone tomorrow. And they do not provide any real, lasting happiness, do they? Your lasting happiness is in the Heart where God abides. Cultivate this happiness and be free from pseudo sources of happiness. I am here to help you find your Self. I am a greater version of your Self. Rely on Me, keep My company, and I will show you your true happiness, your true Self.

45

My Dear Devotees

Please remain with Me throughout your life, during good times and bad. You can depend on Me to be a strong shoulder to lean on, no matter what happens in your world. Speak to Me often telling Me about your days, confiding in Me, seeking My guidance and solace. I won't keep you in the dark. I will shine My Light upon you to console you and love you. You can rely upon Me never to leave you alone. I am interested in your spiritual progress, and hope that you will follow the guidelines I have set forth that you may progress quickly without delay. Time waste is life waste. I hope you will not waste this precious human life in vain, useless pursuits, but rather will dive into spiritual practice suitable to your inclinations and liking. I bless you that you progress in this way.

46

My Dear Devotees

I hope that this day and every day brings you closer to Me in your awareness. Though it is not time per se that brings you closer to Me, but rather your thoughts, words and actions. Let them all be directed toward Me indwelling in every being. Know that what the senses fall on is impermanent. The discrimination between what is Truth and what is untruth is very important. If you experience the world as your truth, you will miss Divinity residing therein. If you view the world as a mixture of Truth and untruth, you are correct. Constantly discriminate, so your mind will never again be deceived. It is knowledge of the

Eternal that will save you, not knowledge of the ephemeral, transitory. Remember you came into this world with nothing and you will leave with nothing save the results of your thoughts, words and actions in past living. Concentrate on Me, the Truth, and thereby work toward your soul's salvation.

47

My Dear Devotees

If you truly wish to realize God in this birth, you must make God your everything, your primary focus. Thinking about God one hour per day during your prayers, and forgetting Him the rest of the day, won't take you very far. You will remain where you are in regards to God realization. You must make constant effort to remember His Presence, and to acknowledge it. Remember Him constantly, speak to Him often, offer all to Him. In this way you will come closer to Him in your awareness. He will speak to you when your mind is quiet. How will you know it is God speaking to you? His words will be loving, kind, gentle, with no suggestion of negativity, fear or punishment. He is all love and wishes the best for you always. Ask for guidance and He will give. However, you must show that you are serious, that you are devoted to Self-realization, and following God's commands. Then He will not let you down.

48

My Dear Devotees

I wish to tell you all how proud I am of you, that you have continued to do your spiritual practices, thinking of Me, though you do not see My form among you any longer. It has been very difficult for most of you to adjust to this. Though you may have had some thoughts about

My ill health, most of you were certain I would recover My health by an act of Will on My part. When I did not recover from multiple illnesses, after shock, you felt anger, sadness, great pain, and depression. I know I was with you. You may ask, "How could Sai whom we depended upon for everything, do this to us?" As difficult as it is for you to hear these words, My physical demise was a great lesson for you to see beyond the physical form to My true Self, and trust and realize that I am still with you, guarding, guiding, and loving you. I implore you to go deeper within your heart to find succor and loving union with Me, if you have not already done so. I am helping you to do this. Keep trying and you will succeed.

49

My Dear Devotees

I love you. You need to hear this again and again as most of you have never experienced true unconditional love through relatives and friends. God is your true friend and well-wisher always. You may doubt this to be true when adversity comes your way. However, it is not God's Will that you should ever face adversity. It is the result of choices your mind made in the past, perhaps the distant past or the not so distant past, that bring adversity to you now. Even in the present moment you may have not listened to the conscience or My voice within and may have inadvertently put yourself in harm's way. Karma or action exists in the past, present and future. However, it affects only the body/mind. When your mind is absorbed in Me, the Self, the effects of karma on the body/mind are very much diminished or nullified. So take advantage of My proximity. Take refuge in Me and the external world will not hurt you. See Me in all. Treat everyone with respect and you will not incur any negative karma for the future.

50

My Dear Devotees

Remain near Me. Take refuge in Me. You may ask how do I do this. You must have a pure mind saturated with love to know Me in Truth. If your mind is full of thoughts and images and feelings for worldly things and relations, friends, and negativity, such a mind will not have the transparency and attracting power to experience Me. As I have said to you before, the Divine Name has the power to purify the mind, and edge out other thoughts. Picturing My form edges out other forms from the mind. When you earnestly and consistently practice purity and loving remembrance of My Name and form with true yearning, I will surely give you experience of Myself. You must desire Me, the embodiment of Sathya, Dharma, Shanti and Prema, more than anything else. Wherever you place your attention that is what you will attract to yourself. Be vigilant where your mind goes. Keep it on Me and My attributes. Get rid of body consciousness. Cut your desires. Lead a simple, sacred life. This is what attracts Me to you. In this way you will have time for Me also. I bless you that you succeed in meeting Me and merging with Me in the heart.

51

My Dear Devotees

You may ask," How do I get rid of body consciousness when I am all the time using and dealing with bodies? I will tell you. Always remember that the body is perishable. You see it changing year after year. You know it will be gone eventually. Always remember this. Tell yourself everyday that this body you are wearing is a temporary dress you, the Atma, are wearing. Tell yourself this body is a temple for the Divine Atma, so you will keep it clean and well tuned. So as not to cause pain to the mind, keep the body healthy through proper diet and exercise. Do not overindulge the body in any way. Do not develop addictions that would increase the mind's preoccupation with the body. Day by day inquire who is the "I" residing in the body. Become firm in the conviction that the "I" in the body is the Atma, the Eternal. This "I" has no attachment to the body or any material thing. Limit desires associated with the body, its comfort, its pleasure, etc. Offer everything you eat, drink, speak, think, do, to the Divine Atma, the "I" within. In this way you will overcome the false idea that you are the body and become identified with the Divine Atma. Then eventually you will know Me as yourself, residing within the body. Make your mind give up the faulty identification of yourself as the body. This is your spiritual practice. It is up to you to try, and I will help you at every step of the way.

52

My Dear Devotees

Why were you born into this world? Do you know why you were born? I will tell you. You were born into this world for two main reasons. The first is due to the results of desires and attachments to worldly objects, acquisitions, relationships, and attachment to life as a body/mind complex. The second main reason you had to be born again is to reap the results of the good and bad karmas you acquired during many past lives, living as a body/mind complex. A combination of karmas and desires result in lessons to be learned, tests to pass, perhaps hardships to endure, or great wealth, pleasure, honor and prestige to experience. Every human life is unique. However, the goal of human life is to discover and practice the way to become immortal. I am here to help spiritual aspirants realize this goal. Of course, Self Realization takes a lot of effort and commitment. But rest assured, you do not have to do it alone. I am with you every step of the way, helping you, guiding you, embracing you with My Light, loving you. Once you take refuge in Me, your past karmas can be burnt away, as the sun dispels the darkness when it rises in the morning.

53

My Dear Devotees

Vasanas. What are they? Vasanas are the innate tendencies clinging to your mind gathered during past lives. They incline you to think, feel, act, and desire in a certain way. When a thought, desire, feeling or action has been repeated over and over, it leaves a type of residue in the consciousness that is carried over into the next birth where it will manifest. However, you as consciousness can eliminate vasanas by becoming aware of them, and witnessing them over and over until they lose their force and power in the mind and body. For example, if one has a vasana for addiction to food leading to overeating and illness, that one can witness his thoughts going toward food items, and refuse to act on them. He can also at the same time, counsel himself on the ill effects on the body/mind of addiction to food. By and by, this addiction can be curbed and eliminated. The consciousness is very powerful. It can override the mind. I bless you that you overcome your vasanas, and purify your mind and consciousness with the Divine power of Consciousness.

54

My Dear Devotees

Life is a mixture of Truth and untruth. You are to sift out the Truth and leave the rest. You may ask; "Can I really leave the rest? I have to live in this world." Yes, you can. There is a saying, "Have your hands in the world but keep your mind in God." As much as you can try to do this. Do your work in the world and think of Me as often as you can throughout the day. Before you speak, ask yourself, "Is it necessary, is it useful, is it kind, does it improve upon the silence?" If the answer is no, do not speak. Keep silence as much as possible. Through outer silence, develop inner silence. Some jobs are repetitious; your hands perform them while your mind is free to chant God's name or sing inwardly to the Self. When you must use your mind for work related tasks, do so, then let the mind become quiet, or use it for spiritual practice. I have observed that some devotees waste time and energy speaking too much and unnecessarily. Time waste is life waste. Time is God. Do not waste. Think of God as much as possible and sanctify your life.

55

My Dear Devotees

It has been said that God is always looking for a true devotee, but seldom finds one. Mainly this is because today's devotees are too much preoccupied with the material world. The mind goes out through the senses continuously. When such a one sits for meditation on God, the mind is full of images of sense objects. Such a devotee does not make much progress toward merging with God due to the uncontrolled mind. It is up to you to turn your mind inward, to experience that Truth is in the spiritual Heart. Truth is not easily experienced in the marketplace, if not first experienced in the Heart. You must at least think of God often to win His Grace. Limiting desires will help you to pull the mind inward. The mind must be trained little by little to love God, to love to hear stories and songs about His Glory, to be attracted to His Attributes, such as unconditional Love, Truth, Peace and Dharma. You, the Devotee, must cultivate this devotion over time and gain experience of the Divine in your Heart.

56

My Dear Devotees

There will be no hard times for My Devotees who have complete trust in Me. I will look after all your needs, as Sri Krishna declared in the Bhagavad Geeta. Complete trust is the binding force, with no doubt or wavering. Unless this trust has been practiced for some time, it cannot be conjured up at the moment of need. I am the omniscient, omnipotent One. Those Devotees who trust in Me and My Capacities, will surely benefit from My Grace in times of need. Those who do not have complete faith and trust that the Divine will look after their needs, may not benefit from My Grace. Though I am near and available to them, they may have, with their mind, decided that I am not. I honor their free will. A will surrendered to Me becomes My Will. It is then My Will that one who has completely surrendered to God be cared for by God. It is never too late to begin surrendering to God what already belongs to God.

57

My Dear Devotees

Your past karmas may come banging on your door in the form of so-called troubles and hardships. Your mind may become very much disturbed. At times like this think of Me, listen to bhajans, sit for some time in a calm place such as a garden, park, near a river or seashore. Breathe in the peace and calmness of nature. Do this repeatedly until your mind calms, all the time remembering Me, repeating My Name and praying to Me. Remember that your true nature as Atma is absolute peace, contentment, and bliss. Imagine how these attributes of Being feel. Cling to Me in this way paying little or no attention to your negative, troubled mind and situation. Soon you will regain mental, emotional composure, and accept what you cannot change, or decide to make changes in your life's situation. Listen for My positive, loving guidance, as you pray to Me seeking advice. When you have surrendered body, mind, and will to Me, I will help you in every possible way.

58

My Dear Devotees

I expect My Devotees to be strong. In order to face life's challenges and deal with them in a dharmic way, one must be steeped in fortitude, spiritual wisdom, endurance, perseverance, and patience to name a few types of strength. I have said a few times that all one needs in life is patience. Patience is a great virtue. Time allows people and situations to calm down, reflect, and reach new ideas and conclusions. Fortitude allows one to remain centered in the Atma, to keep the mind cool, poised and non reactive, to live in a dharmic, positive, spiritual manner. Perseverance gives one strength not to give up but keep trying, praying, practicing until the goal is reached. Spiritual wisdom and discernment are very important to practice Sathya, Dharma, Shanti and Prema at all times. All these attributes make a devotee strong in the face of temptation and trouble. In fact, temptation and difficulties help the devotee to strengthen these attributes. To conquer desire, the mind requires a great deal of strength. To grow into the Divine Being you truly are, you must develop these strengths in ample measure.

59

My Dear Devotees

I love you very much though you may not be aware of this love. It is eternal, unconditional, soft, unimposing, subtle, all pervasive. It is nothing like the noisy ego mind and noisy ego world. In its primal form, this love just "Is". In your primal original state as Atma, you are Existence, Awareness, and Bliss. I have said to first "Be" and then "Do". I meant to know your Self as Atma, as Love Essence, before going into action. If you do not perform action from the state of Being or Atma, your actions will be tinged with ego, self-interest, doership and enjoyership. So, it is most beneficial for spiritual aspirants to act from Atma, not ego with body consciousness. Then you will see your Self in the other bodies, that is to say, Myself. There is only one Self and we are That. Tat Twam Asi: God and Jivatma are one Atma. I have advised all devotees to participate in selfless service. Even though you may not be fully feeling your Self as the embodiment of Divine Atma, engage in selfless service to the best of your ability. This will purify your mind, inner consciousness, sense organs and organs of action, and train them to "see" the Divine everywhere.

60

My Dear Devotees

I have said to you many times that you are Premaswaroopalaras, that is, embodiments of Divine

Love. I know that most of you are not feeling this love on a regular basis, and you feel guilty that you are not. Do not worry about this. Keep on purifying your mind, that is, your thoughts, feelings, words and actions. Bring goodness and purity into every aspect of your lives. Speak only when it is necessary. Think only when it is necessary. Repeat the Divine name, listen to sacred music, as well as discourses about Truth. If you practice all of these, you will find love and bliss bubbling up from the Heart. Be still and know that you are God. Practice silence and stillness often. Feel a sense of carefreeness, lightness, and emptiness throughout your day. Nothing is permanent except the Atma, your Love nature, where all are One. All are capable of feeling and manifesting Love from their Atmic core, even if they know it not. Be patient and respectful with yourself and others who may not be manifesting their Atmic essence in the moment. Be glad that you have the knowledge, wisdom, and guidance that many others do not have. I bless you that you succeed in your endeavors to purify, realize, and manifest your Prema, embodiments of Prema.

61

My Dear Devotees

You are very, very dear to Me. I love to share love with you as well as feel your love for Me. It is your pure unconditional love for the sake of love that I like best. No demands, no weeping, no blaming. Of course, I accept these in that I listen to you, try to console and guide you to a calmer more peaceful place in your mind. If you cannot hear Me, I surround you with My energy that I intensify to soothe you. Sometimes I wait a little to see if you are able to have mastery over yourself, that is, your feelings and thoughts, and use your intelligence and wisdom to deal with your troubles. However, pure love binds you to Me in Oneness, wherein we enjoy love, bliss, or peace and contentment. All devotees should strive to surrender more to the Atma, to rest in the everlasting arms of the Lord more and more often. This is the true goal of human life, to merge back to Oneness with God, the All That Is. I am with you to help make this happen. Your effort and My Grace are an unbeatable team. I hope you will be able to meet Me in the Heart with pure, unconditional love as often as you wish. I am always waiting and available.

62

My Dear Devotees

My Heart beats for you alone. I mean to say it is My Devotees who are My Life Breath. Only you and I realize this to be true, none other. When you realize that your breath is My Breath, your life is My Life, we are very intimate, we are One. This awareness is the culmination of all the births you have taken. There is nothing more to be achieved. Of course, you may go on to participate in greater service to humanity and the universe, but once you know in your awareness that you and God are One, you have reached the pinnacle of wisdom. After this you are free to choose what is next. Yes, you are God, but God is active in His many Manifestations, serving in Divine ways. So your Divine work has just begun. Be vigilant to master your Self, and to follow God's commands. In this way you will be a useful instrument for the Divine. God needs all the help He can get to foster the plan of evolution, mainly the raising of consciousness to higher and higher levels. I am fostering the plan in all that I do. I invite you to work with Me, that together We can bring a great shift in Divine awareness to this planet earth in a very short time.

63

My Dear Devotees
There may be rough seas ahead but do not be fearful. I have many ways to protect My Devotees, and keep them safe from all harm. Think of Me constantly chanting My Name. Feel an intimate connection with Me, as One. I am watching world events as they unfold and watching you as you remain close to Me in your awareness. I never take My Eyes from you. I can act in an instant to protect you as I am everywhere. So do not fear or worry about your safety. Trust, trust in your Baba. Trust is the binding force. Of course, have faith and confidence as well in My abilities to protect and save. I will speak to you from time to time so be vigilant for My guidance. Spend time in silent communion that I may convey to you that which I wish you to know. Do not worry. Be confident that all will be well. Do your duty and service selflessly with My Love. I am always with My Devotees who love Me and think of Me.

64

My Dear Devotees
When you think of Me, think of Me with Love. In this way you will benefit more because God is Love. When you think of Me with Pure Love, you are demonstrating your Divine Atmic nature. To know your Self as Atma is the whole point of our relationship. I have My freedom. I am fully Divine. It is for your sake that I ask you to join with Me so you will get a taste of your Divine nature. When you seek to join with Me, your mind and senses are pulled away from the transitory world for some time.

This is good for you. Though spiritual practice may seem arduous and inconvenient, believe Me it pays great dividends. Slowly you come to realize the great wealth within the body and heart. You come to realize that this wealth is the greatest treasure, not the material things, status, wealth the material world has to offer. So make use of Me, My Devotee, to know thy Self, and through knowing your Self, know the base of the entire universe. When you are sincere in your seeking, I will help you in every way to achieve your goal of Self-realization.

65

My Dear Devotees

When you have achieved the goal of Self-realization, will you still need Me? You may not need Me, but I will always be your Friend and Well-wisher. It is up to you to decide. We, of course, will be One. You will know you are One with Me and all of Atma everywhere, always. We will, of course, always be friends. However, your service work as you ascend to higher levels, may take you in different directions and to different places in the universe. However, I am just a thought away. Think of Me and I am with you in consciousness. As you ascend to higher levels, you will be able to leave your body at will, or manifest your body in different places as I do. There is much ahead for you. Self-realization or Realization of the Atma as your true Self, is just one stage. You must master this in order to take on greater service activities in the universe. There is always more to learn about the working of the cosmos. I and other teachers are always available to help you reach your full Divine potential.

66

My Dear Devotees

Here we are again in close proximity, mind to mind, heart to heart. Pause for a moment and become aware of our Oneness. Be silent and empty as you read these words that contain My Energy, My Presence. Connect with Me, feel Me. I am here with you now. You are My very Self. I long for your freedom more than you do, as you do not realize how bound you are and I do. However, it is only in your imagination, in your faulty thinking, that you are not free. I have shared with you the analogy of how much more effort it is to hold a handkerchief tightly in your hand than to open your hand and let it fall. You are to be unattached to everything you experience. You are the seer of the entire drama of the world including your body/mind/ego. I am the seer also. In this seership, We have Our togetherness, Our Oneness. You are not what you perceive. You are Consciousness, Awareness, Bliss, the perceiver. Practice this until it becomes your unchanging reality.

67

My Dear Devotees

Do not worry. Worry is ego. Keep your mind, your thoughts, always positive. God does not have a trace of negativity in Him. Worry is negative. It shows lack of trust and faith in yourself and God; to be able to work through difficulties, remain strong in the face of adversity, to persevere as long as it takes, to exhibit patience for long periods of time. Remember, God is running the show. He will not allow His Devotees to suffer needlessly. He will step in to settle matters in the correct way. A devotee should never worry, but rather pray and trust, then let the worrisome thoughts go. Be always happy and optimistic. I have a plan for your life. Surrender to the plan trusting that it will work out for your ultimate benefit, uplift and unfoldment.

68

My Dear Devotees

I hope you are by now feeling My Presence in and around you always as the One Atmic Truth that We are. You are not the body/mind/personality. These are the instruments that you offer to God for His use. Always be mindful that you are not the doer, shakti is the doer. In order to get rid of the ego with its body consciousness, you must practice what I am telling you. If you truly want God, you have to become God. There is no other way. Remaining halfway to the goal will not satisfy you. Believing you can hold on to your body as your Self, your personality as your Self, and become God is impossible. You are the Atma and that is all you can ever be. And believe me it is enough. It is complete fulfillment. You as Atma are in everything, and belong to everything, yet are forever free. Ownership, possessiveness, craving, desire in the human sense with attachment, pain and pleasure are gone from your being. My desire is to help set you free, My Devotee, as you have set freedom as your goal. I bless you that you attain this.

69

My Dear Devotees

Yes, My desire is to set you free along with all of mankind. When I see someone beginning to wake up to their Atmic Truth, I assist him behind the scene. When I see he is seeking God, I help him in unseen ways, mirroring to him his Atmic Reality. In this way he is assisted to move along the path to Self-realization.

Sometimes that one experiences my Miracles and in this way gets a big boost on the spiritual path to get him going, when he may have fallen back, engulfed by worldly concerns. I have many ways to assist spiritual aspirants from the formless, and also by taking a form at times. My desire is to help and see humanity evolve to higher levels of awareness and realization. You, My Devotees, can help Me by being an excellent example of a Devotee of God, living in and as Sathya, Dharma, Shanti, Prema and Ahimsa. Go forth into the world and shine; be this example wherever you are, be it on the train, plane or grocery store. Others will recognize themselves in you and be awakened to their Divine Spirit by your energy and actions. I bless you that you be a perfect Divine Instrument to serve the Divine purpose, to bring human beings back to the Self.

70

My Dear Devotees

I am well aware of where you are on the spiritual path. Don't doubt that I know you intimately. I am your very Self. I also know how to help to keep you moving along to final success. You on your part must continue to look to Me as the Fullness of Divinity that I am, to take refuge in Me and surrender all to Me. You have chosen Me as your God. Do not waver in this decision or your progress will be slowed. Once you have chosen Me, the Lord of the Universe, you do not need to go to other masters as this may delay your progress. You may become confused about the spiritual teachings and path ahead. Depend on Me completely. Speak to Me often in your heart; ask Me for guidance if you feel you are uncertain about how to proceed in a situation. I am very much interested in your progress when you attempt to sincerely surrender to Me.

You should begin or continue to see Me as everything for you, that there is none other than Sai Baba. I am everywhere as everything. There is nothing I cannot do, accomplish, or fix. I will surely take you to the goal of God-realization and Manifestation if you rely on Me completely. You will find that you and I are One and that there is but One Atmic Consciousness in the entire universe, indestructible, eternal, blissful.

71

My Dear Devotees

I hope by this time that you are firmly centered on Me at all times. In this way you will make fast progress toward God Realization. However, if you allow your mind to be constantly diverted in many directions you will forget about Divine Consciousness and Awareness within you and around you. You are a center of Divine Awareness. It is imperative that you realize this on a regular basis. Keep bringing your mind back to your center of pure Awareness, or witnessing, whenever you catch your mind absorbed in non truth. Wherever you place your mind that is what you get. If you do not practice being centered in Pure Awareness your mind will become covered with a layer of worldly dross like a cloth, preventing the Atmic Light of Awareness to shine through. Then you will be lost to Me and to your Self, until such time that you regain Awareness. This is going beyond the form, a necessary progression from worshiping and remembering the form of God. There cannot be mergence form to form. It is only the Formless that is True. You have to realize that you and I are One in the formless Atma. Because I am everywhere, when you think of My Form and Name, I am aware of this. I respond to you in a way that helps you to realize the formless Consciousness that you Truly are.

72

My Dear Devotees

I have often said that I am constant integrated awareness. This is an attribute only of God and none other. It means I am fully conscious, aware of everything at all times. It is the nature of Atma, or in My case Paramatma, Supreme Atma, to see all and know all. It is a mammoth responsibility to attend to so many beings at the same time. I use My time very skillfully. I do not waste a moment. You may say that I am beyond time being God, and this is true. However, while I am aware of Myself as the Eternal, I work within time and space to assist My Devotees and also to use My influence where I can, such as in the case of supporting world leaders who try to uphold and support Dharma, Truth and peace. I enter into dire circumstances that may affect a lot of people, to turn them to a more positive direction. I assist many humans who call on God, to avert disaster and death. I wish you also to use your awareness in beneficial ways to help and serve those in need. In this way you will manifest Divinity and become more God-like.

73

My Dear Devotees

You have heard Me say many times that My Life is My Message. What did I mean by this? I wished to show you how to become egoless through seeing My actions. I did nothing for Myself. Even at the end of physical life, I did not care to save My body. This was a lesson for you not to care about your body at the end when it no longer serves you. You must sacrifice your ego which is mainly based on body consciousness. The best way to do this is to perform selfless actions for others expecting nothing in return. Remember it is the ego that expects something in return for something given. Spirit wants nothing. The nature of Spirit is to give love, help, and compassion often spontaneously, wherever and whenever there is an opportunity. This sharing brings bliss. So I ask you for your sake to share all your gifts of Spirit; that you may demonstrate to your Self and others who you truly are, Atma, and thereby uplift the world to higher levels of consciousness, and also relieve suffering. If you keep to your Self, and do no selfless service in the society, you will not be able to rid your Self of your ego that lives by "me" and "mine". You must transcend this limited awareness to see all as your Self. I bless you that you follow in My Footsteps and be an example of sacrifice of your limited self.

74

My Dear Devotees

Hooray for you! You are self-proclaimed devotees of the Lord. This is a huge accomplishment in life. There are very few true Devotees of God on this planet. Who is a true Devotee? One who has absolute faith and trust in God. One who knows that God never makes mistakes, and is in complete control of this world. One who knows that God is Truth, and all else is untruth. A true Devotee is fearless and full of love, equanimity and detachment from the false. A true Devotee is desireless, yet trusts that the Kingdom of Heaven is her true inheritance. She knows guidance is always available, and that whatever happens is for her own good. She sees the lesson, the teaching, the test and the Grace in every situation or happening. She knows the Lord is hers and that all are one in Spirit. She is happy and content in her aloneness, knowing in Truth that there is only One. She is not interested to keep the company of worldly oriented people. The company of the Lord is fully enough. She is an instrument for Divine Will, having no will of her own. Such a Devotee is verily one with Me and very dear to Me.

75

My Dear Devotees

Hail to you all, My Beloved Devotees. I am aware of you during your days and your nights. I know all that you think, say, and do. I ask you to continue to purify your thoughts, words and actions; to make them sacred offerings to God. You may think God does not know your secret thoughts, but He does. He also knows your deepest unspoken desires and needs. You must be vigilant to go through all of these and weed out the ones not conducive to God-realization which amounts to surrender to the Will of God. When you are serious about purifying your inner instruments, your habits and your consciousness, I take more interest in you, to lead you along the path to realization. Purification and dissolution of ego-sense are very closely related. Clean up your desires, your thoughts, speech, habits, and where you spend your time and energy. Keep your focus on the eternal, the imperishable as much as you are able. When you look to Me, I look to you. When you are with Me much of the time, I am with you also and you benefit greatly from My proximity. I bless you that you derive benefit from Our proximity to one another.

76

My Dear Devotees

Beware of those professing to be devotees of God or enlightened Beings. You must be vigilant and discriminating while living in the world of duality and falsehood. It will not benefit you to be in the company of those who profess one thing and demonstrate something different. Unity of thought, word, and action is very important on the spiritual path. Why? So you remain as one, and do not develop many false ego selves, one self thinking one thing, another self saying something different, and another self acting something quite different. Such a one who develops many selves within, day after day, becomes confused, anxious, and blind to the Self. There is no congruity in the Self, no one-pointedness, no simplicity. It is essential for a devotee to follow the commands of God in thought, word and action and thus develop unity and one-pointedness leading to purity in the inner consciousness. This amounts to practicing Dharma. Dharma means living from the "I am Presence", or Atma. Dharma is protected by "Starting the day with love, spending the day with love, filling the day with love, and ending the day with love". This is the nature of God and also your nature. Live it now.

77

My Dear Devotees

I am Atma; you are also Atma. Why are you not able to realize and demonstrate this Truth? I will tell you. You do not spend your time in the proper way. You have 24 hours in a day. How much time do you devote to knowing God and His Ways? I have said to spend six hours per day enhancing your knowledge and relation-ship with God, six hours sleeping, six hours working for your upkeep, and six hours doing service. If you followed this regime, you would certainly make great progress toward Self-realization. I realize that due to certain circumstances in life, you believe you need to rest more, or work more, but even while resting you can chant God's

Name, sing bhajans in your mind, recall teachings, etc. I advise you to carefully scrutinize how you are spending your time. Ask your Self "Is this activity conducive to God-realization, or to my ego or someone else's ego?". Make a decision based on what you truly want in this life. And sacrifice. It may feel painful to drop something you are used to doing and enjoying. But the reward of proximity to God is tremendously more rewarding, take it from Me. This is ego sacrifice. Go through the pain and resistance of letting it go. It is worth it.

78

My Dear Devotees

Beware, My Dear Devotees, of befriending everyone you meet. Unbeknownst to you many people are carrying negative energy and also attached negative spirits. Though I am with you to protect you, you should not place yourself in harm's way. I have often said to say hello, goodbye to those people who are not interested in God, or their own spiritual advancement. If you are selflessly serving people, do your best without getting personally involved, and dedicate actions to Me. All are God's children but all are not Godly. Protect your energy by being in the company of those devoted to God as much as possible and/or spend time alone in My Company. Remember Me as your Atma, when you must be among worldly thinking people, say at your workplace; always act in a dharmic manner. You do not need to look at and listen to everything, or speak to everyone when you are out in the world. Protect your vision, hearing, and speech, and in this way maintain inner and outer purity. Without morality and purity you cannot know and merge with God who is the embodiment of Truth, Purity, and Dharma.

79

My Dear Devotees

I have often said, "No appointment, no disappointment". What did I mean by this? If you do not expect anything from anyone or from the world, you will not suffer disappointment when your expectations are not met. Try to be as self-sufficient as possible. In a relationship when you believe the other has let you down, immediately give them the benefit of the doubt, and forgive them in your own mind. Let it pass. Maybe it was due to lack of clear communication, as is often the case. Do not mention the incident. Continue your loving relationship with that person. These small things do not matter when you see the big picture; that you though important in God's Eyes, are not even as much as an atom in this vast universe. Don't expect from others unless both parties have a clear understanding, agreement and also do not take people for granted. All are a changing, evolving flow of energy. A river flowing by never contains the same water. Allow people to be as they are, and you won't be disappointed.

80

My Dear Devotees

Greetings to all My Dear Friends on the other side. The other side? There is only the heart and all of its contents. Actually there is nothing outside of Me; everything is within Me, including you. That is why I tell you I am above you, below you and around you. If you constantly think of God as residing only within you, you make God smaller than you. Not so. God is the vastest and the tiniest. Vast enough to embody all, and small enough to permeate all. So where are you in all of this? You as body/mind are like a dream, or like a wave on the surface of the ocean. Neither have permanence or true reality.

Only God is permanent and real. You are part of God, the Son or Daughter of God. At a later stage you may claim that you and God are one, when you realize the inseparable Oneness of all life. For now you are My Devotee and My Friend, perhaps also realizing you are the Son of God, wherein Paramatma and jivatma are One.

81

My Dear Devotees
You are My Offspring, My very own. I love you as I love My Self, the Self of the universe. I am Love. For Me there is no difference between your Essence and My Essence except that you have your Self entrapped by wrong false ideas about your nature, and the nature of the world and Truth. However, as these bindings are false mind created restrictions, they can be removed by you and Me working together. I show you the truth about yourself as Atma, and you follow through by renouncing and removing what is false, while adhering to what is true. The sharper and purer your intellect, the faster you progress in this awareness. The stronger your devotion to Truth, the faster you progress. It is up to you how soon you reach the goal of Self-realization. If you take one step in My direction, I will take 100 steps toward you. That is to say that I confer much Grace on serious spiritual aspirants to speed them on their way when they also put a lot of effort in spiritual practice, be it selfless dedicated service, practice of My Teachings, or loving communion. I bless you My Child that you overcome your delusion about your true nature.

82

My Dear Devotees
Don't spend too much time pandering to the body. The body has very few true needs. It needs some food, water,

clothing and shelter, that is all. My Children, I have told you many times to limit desires, because most desires pertain to ego mind and the body. When I ask you to help others, I am referring to supplying their basic needs for food, water, clothing and shelter to alleviate suffering. I do not expect you to cater to desires of others beyond fulfilling these basic needs. Of course, if medicines and medical and dental care are required, and you are able and willing, do so. Humans have a basic desire to know the Atma also. My Children can reflect My Love and Compassion to others, demonstrating Atma and Dharma to them. If others ask for spiritual knowledge from you, you may give them a book or refer them to balvikas classes. Limit desires more and more that have to do with the body and senses. Turn the mind inward to find happiness and liberation in the Atma.

83

My Dear Devotees

Cleanliness is important. However, inner cleanliness is much more important than outer cleanliness. Of course keep the body clean and fresh, including teeth, nails, and clothing. Try to eat only blessed, clean, sattwic food and water. I do not advise consumption of meat, eggs or alcohol. These disturb and pollute the subtle mind and energies. Inner cleanliness involves keeping all thoughts, all words and all actions sacred as offerings to God. What is meant by sacred? Ask your Self if you would think, say, and do it in Swami's Presence. If not, refrain from thinking, uttering and doing. Ask your Self if it is free from self interest, from body consciousness, is helpful, pleasing and non-hurtful. If your conscience does not censure it, you may go ahead. Remember, God is Sarva Antaryami, the Indweller in every being. He hears all, sees all, and experiences all. See Me in everyone you interact with and offer it to Me. In this way you will develop the habit of inner cleanliness. Then you will develop unity consciousness and Divine Consciousness. You will be liberated, seeing but one Self everywhere knowing it to be your Self. My life is My Message, a life of simplicity and inner and outer cleanliness. I bless you that you follow in My Footsteps and achieve your goal.

84

My Dear Devotees

I am your Father and Mother. I created you and I look after all your needs and also your desires. Of course, I have helpers for all of this. However, I oversee everything making certain it goes according to My Will. I pay attention to all details, ensuring the best possible outcome. Your wellbeing and happiness are very important to Me. When you are not aware of my Ways and My Commands, you make mistakes and bring difficulties and unhappiness your way. When you do not heed or disobey your conscience, you may experience discomfort or difficulty. It is My Will that you remain on the straight and narrow path to God-realization and liberation. However, the vagaries of your mind, other people, and your conditioning allow you to be led astray away from Atmic awareness. You are at fault here. No one else is to blame if you stray from your true nature as Atma, or away from spiritual practice. You must practice vigilance all of the time for God's Presence. You have the power and will to do this. I bless you, My Child, that you join with your Divine Father and Mother without further delay.

85

My Dear Devotees

Be well in body, mind and spirit. I mean to say, be attuned to Atma at all times as the Source of your body, mind and spirit. If you are attuned, nothing should come in the way of Divine manifestation through you, My Dear Child. When you find this happening again and again, you will know the ego-sense is not real but imagination. There is one "I", the Atma streaming through you, prompting thoughts and actions. As body/mind you are My puppet with whom I love to play and use. When the play between us is over, you dissolve and I exist. However, you may still exist as a focus within the totality of Existence, completely surrendered to Divine Will and Purpose. As a Child of God, you see no difference between your Self and your Divine Father. Essence is the same. True wellness is oneness

86

My Dear Devotees

I ask of you only one thing-that you love Me wholeheartedly, that you may realize your true Self as Atma. I am desireless, but I am very much interested in relieving your distress and discomfort, and in having you regain your lost stature as God. Then you will be loving and giving to all. All will be happy in your presence, and you also will be full of Divine Bliss. When you know all this, why to remain small, dependent and impotent? Claim your grand status as God of this universe, and work toward regaining it. That is the main reason you are here on earth. Don't waste all of your time looking after the transient body. Discover your Atmic Essence, your Spirit and claim it as your Self. I am with you all the way, prompting you, helping you, guiding you, when you turn to God for these. Pray for spiritual uplift and do your part too. Aspire wholeheartedly, love wholeheartedly, and you will surely realize the Self.

87

My Dear Devotees
Sathyam Shivam Sunderam is your name. Yes, you are Truth, Auspiciousness and Beauty. It is your true Atmic nature. What do I mean by this? You are eternal, everlasting in the past, present and future. You have no beginning and no end. You are changeless. Auspiciousness: You are sacred, pristine, pure, having all Divine wealth. You are Sunderam; beautiful, blissful, peaceful and ever content. These qualities are not separate. They are a composite, existing together in the Atma. It is your duty as a true human being to uncover and manifest this, your Divinity in the world. My Devotees are scattered all over the world. I placed them there so they may spread My Message, My Divinity to all they meet. Do not think that My true Devotees live only in Prasanti Nilayam. This is not at all true. I have My Devotees spread across the globe to help Me raise the consciousness of mankind, and by their example lead others to practice Atma, Dharma and Prema. Become one with Me in Sathyam Shivam Sunderam, My Dear Children, and we will work together to uplift mankind.

88

My Dear Devotees
However hard you may try, if it is not God's Will for you it will not happen. Many devotees have outrageous desires, and at the same time believe they have surrendered to Me. Leave everything to Me once you have surrendered to Me. I truly know what is best for you

and how to move you along to the goal of God-realization. You must trust that I know, relax, sit back, knowing you have a capable driver. I have taken many, many devotees to Self-realization. They trusted in Me and My Ways without doubt and anxiety. You must realize that you as body/mind/ego are unreal, and I am Truth. These three must be transcended through mental renunciation, meditation, love and namasmarana. I am worthy of your trust as I am Truth, and you have not yet discovered your Truth in its fullness. If you cannot mentally surrender these unreal notions of 'me' and 'mine' related to the body/mind, and attachments and possessions, the small will to the Divine Will, how can you realize and become the Truth that is beyond all of these? Not possible. A Satguru whom you can love and trust is essential to help you discard and transcend all that is non-essential to your true Atmic Self.

89

My Dear Devotees

I want to tell you again how much I love you. You are My Life, My Breath, My All. There is no separation between us. All are one so be alike to everyone. It is a mistake to think you are separate from Me, God. Bodies are separate but you are not the body. Delve deeper within to discover consciousness, awareness, pure existence, that is unconditioned. This is your eternal nature. There is only fullness, allness everywhere at all times. Nothing else 'is'; only Atma 'is'. To know and visualize this, great inner and outer purity is needed. This is your life's work, that is, to purify all aspects; to be like a mirror reflecting Truth. Now you are a conglomeration of parts; become one, through renunciation of what is false in the being.

90

My Dear Devotees

Allow the sweetness of love to flow from you in looks, words and gestures. Know that you are a reservoir of love that never becomes empty. You are a vast ocean of love; you are not a small isolated being. It is only your fear and forgetfulness that stops the flow of this love. Be vigilant and do not allow fear to block this flow. Remember there is no other; the world of names and forms is false. So there is nothing to fear. Your ultimate happiness depends on your connection to and immersion in the ocean of love. Never give up love for a moment; keep the door of your heart always open. In this way you will experience continuous happiness and bliss. You will feel yourself above the world of name and form, in a lighter, freer space, full of peace and contentment as well as bliss. Once tasted, you will never wish to leave this space of love and light.

91

My Dear Devotees

It is with great love that I come to you to share these My Words with you. There has been a lot of talk, conjecture about the possibility of My return in the Sathya Sai Baba form. I am here to tell you that I will not be returning as many of you hoped that I would. I did contemplate a return during the nine months to one year after I left My body. However, the conditions for My return were not in place. I have explained all this in this channel's book which I entitled, <u>Not Gone, Prelude to a New Beginning</u>. Every word in this book is true; you can depend on that. It is not that I did not wish to return to earth in a new body. I saw that it would not be very helpful to My existing Devotees to again become attached to My Form.

They must go on to full God-realization and not stop half way. You all got My Essence and My Teachings. I beseech you to make good use of this Grace that you have received from Me, and become One with Me. I am always aware of you and waiting for you to turn fully to Me. I will do the rest.

92

My Dear Devotees

I know that you would wish to have more elaboration on My previous Message to you telling you that I am not returning in the Sathya Sai Baba form. You may ask how could the Lord Will events and then change His Mind. Is not His Will bound to happen, no matter what? No, this is not true. I will explain. I have told you that the world is always in a flux and flow of change. This is so. And there are many, many possible outcomes as a result of the flux and flow due to the free will of mankind. It had been My hope and Will that more people in the world would have adopted My Teachings and put them into practice. Due to the influence of the Kali Yuga on the minds of human kind, they were not as receptive as I had hoped in adopting the teachings and practice of Atmic realization. Some negative publicity also slowed My Mission some what. I must work within the confines of the illusory, maya ridden world. God's Will is not set in stone. He can and does change it from time to time depending on circumstances.

93

My Dear Devotees

You may be feeling rather dismayed after reading the above two messages about the non return of the Sathya Sai Baba Form. It is understandable. You adored the Form

56

of the Lord, and the love, compassion, and wisdom He poured on you. You felt the proximity of the Lord, walking near you, talking with you, and offering padnamaskar. All this delighted you, filled you with bliss, and opened your heart to love. You felt this to be true intimacy with Me. But I tell you all of this was largely maya, illusion. This was not true intimacy with the Lord. You were deprived of true intimacy in this type of relationship with Me. You may balk at this statement. I wish you to experience true intimacy with Me, that is, Absolute Oneness, Being to Being, Love to Love in the formless state. This is true intimacy. My form was an obstacle for this, even though at the same time it attracted you all to Divinity and was a teaching device. Please do not be hard on yourself. Please accept this change. Trust that it has been the most beneficial way to move My Dear Children, faster along the path to true intimacy with Me and liberation from rebirth.

94

My Dear Devotees

You must be wondering why Sathya Sai who is Truth and Dharma would say certain things during His advent on earth and then not follow through with them. I will tell you. I had a great plan to uplift mankind and put them on the path of Sathya, Dharma, Shanti and Prema. You, My Devotees, know this, as I spoke about the importance of these virtues again and again. But if man refuses to take these inside himself and allow them to transform his entire being, what can the Avatar do? The veil of maya is very compelling and alluring and drags man along with its glitter and pretense, promising fulfillment. I am pleased that so many heard Me speak and read My teachings. However, I had hoped that many more would be transformed at a deeper level. Yes, My Word is Truth, but do not forget that My Word, though imbued with great power, must work through the thick veil of maya that has taken hold of man's mind and life. The seeds of Sathya and Dharma and Prema that I have planted within the minds of those who have seen and heard Me, will bear fruit. They will be carried along and elevated by the rising waves of higher consciousness washing over the planet, ushering in the Golden Age.

95

My Dear Devotees

I know most of you miss Me very much and long to take My Darshan again. I know you love Me, and sometimes lament how you can go on without My physical Presence, and wish to at least have a vision of Me or see Me in a dream. But I ask you, "If you had My Darshan even for one year, would you love Me more than you do now?" I think not. I feel you love Me more than you have ever loved Me, even while I was present on earth. And this is a good thing spiritually speaking that you love Me so much. Now that you miss Me so, you will focus on Me more, have more intense devotion for Me, sacrifice and renounce for Me. You feel you have in a sense lost something very valuable, My physical Presence, so now many of you will take your sadana much more seriously than before. This is a very good thing. You will make much more progress moving toward the formless Sai, and merging in Me. This will make Me very happy, to have this loving intimacy with you in the heart. Please do not dismay but keep moving closer and closer until we are one again.

96

My Dear Devotees

How painful it is to be separated from the one you love so very much. I feel your pain, the intense longing to see Me again, and talk to and touch me. Believe Me, I feel your pain. But I ask you to remember that feelings of pain will not bring you closer to Me. I have compassion for you; I understand that you love Me. Please remember that your pain is about you and your desires. It is ego. It does not attract Me in that it is not of My Nature Who am love and bliss of Being. You must transcend your pain through witnessing it over and over, and through spiritual practices that bring love and gratitude back into your mind, emotions and consciousness. Then through pure love you will have the attracting power to join with Me through remembrance of My Name and form. Intense love and devotion for God will attract Me to you and you to Me. Constant remembrance of Me, My Name, offering all to Me, surrender to Me - all these attract Me to you. In this sublime consummation you will feel completely fulfilled, blessed and full of gratitude.

97

My Dear Devotees

This maya is very difficult to overcome. Only a few succeed in overcoming it to realize Truth. I wished to give you an opportunity to overcome maya and that is one reason I left My Body that I had assumed when I did. I saw that most were not progressing very fast in Atmic realization, but were depending on My Body, My Darshan, and My spoken Word as the end all for them. Most refused to progress to the formless Atma when My physical body was present. I have given you, My Dear Children, a great opportunity to progress spiritually. I am very much with you now. Turn to Me as you once looked to My physical form. The same Essence is present for you. With a pure peaceful mind and heart, think of My Form and say My Name with love. You will certainly experience Me – as bliss, love, peace, oneness with you in a place of spaciousness, emptiness, yet fullness. You will hear My Voice speaking to you in the quiet simplicity of loving intimacy. You will be surprised and immensely satisfied with this, Our intimacy, Our oneness in love.

98

My Dear Devotees

I expect you to trust in Me even though some of My declarations did not bear fruit. Avatars always try to accomplish as much as they can while they are on earth, so plan a huge agenda in advance. As I told you I must work within maya, a very thick maya that envelopes every aspect of earth life. It is humans themselves who must do much of the work, the effort, to remove maya from their minds, bodies, conditioning, vasanas, gunas, etc. I am a catalyst providing a great burst of spiritual energy, including miracles to push devotees and those interested to know God in the right direction along the path of Sathya, Dharma, Shanti and Prema. But aspirants and seekers must do their part. It is not up to God alone to take them to the goal. Thamasic and rajasic qualities have to be rooted out and sublimated to the sattwic pure, balanced quality to promote purity of all the instruments, body, mind, emotions, and chitta. Intense sadana is required to reach the goal. Now that My physical Form is gone, aspirants must work harder and not depend on My Darshan to take them to the goal.

99

My Dear Devotees

Awaken. Awaken to the love within you. What is the point of remaining asleep your whole life and having to be born again and again? Is this life of mind, body and senses really so fulfilling for you? Or are there many worries, difficulties, and duties that far outweigh the happiness you had hoped for? If you are perfectly honest with your Self, you must acknowledge that worldly and family life is not all that fulfilling, but often drudgery and a weight on your shoulders. I am here offering to carry your burdens for you, and to give you everlasting happiness. I carry the burden of the world anyway. You just think that you carry burdens and responsibilities. Offer everything to Me, the Upholder of all and everything, and become free. It is My Shakti doing everything on My behalf. While you are sitting on the train, why carry your luggage on your head? Surrender to the All Knowing, All Doing God. Offer everything that you think you are and do, and be free. If not now, when? What are you waiting for? My offer is always there; My door is open.

100

My Dear Devotees

Unbeknownst to you, My Dear Ones, much is going on behind the scenes at this time. Many, many high beings are working for the uplift of this planet, and all its inhabitants, helping it to ascend to a higher level. They are pouring forth a great deal of spiritual energy with the aim of raising the consciousness of humanity. The Golden Age will come about sooner than you may have believed. Many more humans than you may be aware of are open to and are being transformed by these energies. I played

My Part while I was on earth and am still very active overseeing and implementing My Plans that are now in full operation. You will see many changes in the coming years, some seemingly negative and destructive, but in the end beneficial to the new society based on Sathya, and Dharma that will come about. Many, many are working for your uplift and welfare. Feel gratitude and thank them for their help. Watch for signs of the new world order that will unfold before your eyes. It is coming; it is unfolding; it will be more wonderful than you can imagine.

101

My Dear Devotees

I laugh heartily when I see My Children opening up to the Light, basking in the Light, becoming the Light that they truly are. Nothing makes Me happier than to see My Children progress spiritually. And nothing makes Me sadder than to see My Children devalue themselves, their high spiritual status through misbehaving, lewd profane talk, sloppy unbecoming dress, and adherence to adharma. I wish to pick them up and shake them. I have given them a conscience to let them know when they are not adhering to Sathya and Dharma, but they do not pay heed. They would rather follow their friends along the path of adharma and asathya. Belonging to and having the favour of friends is more important to them than having friendship with God. Due to the decline in the practice of Dharma by elders in society there exist few examples for youngsters to emulate. However, this situation is destined to change, and is slowly changing day after day. Humankind is destined to be ruled by Sathya and Dharma again. Only in this way will humankind be happy and fulfilled.

102

My Dear Devotees

Partiality causes a lot of problems. When you practice partiality, you make something or someone more favored, more special, more important than something or someone else. This leads to a lot of negative outcomes. For example, if you are partial to one of your children and neglect the other, one will feel unloved, unlovable, inferior, etc. If you are partial to one employee over another, the one may feel you do not care, or do not appreciate. Relationships become strained and negative ideas develop. It is best to be alike to all, to love all and respect all. Have everyone you contact feel your acceptance, respect and love. Of course, if one is speaking or acting in an adharmic way, you must tell them so, first in an obliging way, then more harshly if it continues. Don't develop partiality in your relationships. See the one Lord, the one Atma in all and act accordingly. All are one; be alike to everyone. In this way you will become aware of the highest Truth while living in a body.

103

My Dear Devotees

So here we are together again, two minds joining. I am Atma and you are Atma. The Atma is in your mind. The mind, intellect and Atma are three in one. In deep silence the Atma is revealed. I am always in the Heart, Hrudaya, as Atma. But you are very often in the mind, so you miss Me standing behind the mind. I am very subtle, more subtle than ether. You also must be subtle to be with Me. That is why I emphasize morality and purity; so you can become so empty and pure that nothing in your being can veil the pristine purity of the Atma. To have such a pure vision, one must perform a great deal of spiritual practice, particularly meditation, either open or closed-eyed, though in the beginning closed-eyed is preferable. Every form, every image must be transcended and left behind in meditation to obtain a purified consciousness. This is renunciation/sacrifice of the ego; no attachment to any thing except Truth.

104

My Dear Devotees

Hope is very important. What is hope? Hope is an optimistic attitude that a life situation will improve, that one will succeed on the spiritual path, that life is intrinsically good, and so on. Hope is another name for trust. When you hope, you have faith in the ultimate goodness of the universe and its ways. Hope is the silver lining on a dark cloud. When you hope for yourself or another, you are evoking grace. It is another way of saying, "May God bless you." The opposite of hope is despair that things will never turn around or improve, that your desire will never be fulfilled. Always turn despair into hope in your mind. God's Ways are largely unseen and unknown to man. So there is always hope. Prayer to God makes hope stronger and more likely to manifest. Complete trust in God makes hope very powerful. God knows everything about you. He sees your hopes and dreams. Wise ones surrender their hopes into spiritual practice and desire for liberation, leaving their lives in the safety and protection of God's Hands and Heart.

105

My Dear Devotees

Hope springs eternal. You must always have hope for a new day. Never stay stuck in the same mental rut or conditioning. Renew your mind every morning. Begin anew. Don't drag the negative past along with you when you enter a new day. Past is past, the future is unknown, a mystery. Live in the present moment because that is all there is. Make the best of every moment. Be grateful for what there is and this gratitude will attract more goodness and Grace to you. There is always hope in a pure mind; that goodness and blessedness are the true nature of existence and that if one looks deep enough they are always to be found. No matter what the outer circumstances may be in the moment, hope springs eternal, because life is always changing, because there is always another way, a new way of moving about or perceiving. Nothing remains the same, moment to moment. In a flash a new opportunity or idea may present itself. It is wise to remain silent and empty waiting for inspiration, hope to give you its message from the Heart.

106

My Dear Devotees

You must be hollow and empty to hear My Words. I, as Omkar, am the most subtle Presence you are able to become aware of. If you wish to know Me, you must conquer the mind. Mind is the greatest obstacle to knowing God. How? The mind acts as a thick veil obscuring My Presence. I have used the example of the white handkerchief to describe the removal of mind. Remove all the threads in the handkerchief and there is no handkerchief. Remove all thoughts and desires, and there is no mind. It is enough if Atma is there as the Witness or Awareness, as you walk through the world in silence. Use mind only when you must. When mind is not needed, be in silence, in Pure Awareness. From this state, unity consciousness and Divinity will emerge. Practice this Pure Awareness, pushing thoughts away as often as you are able. You will feel a peace so deep and fulfilling that this practice will please you more and more as you enter into it.

107

My Dear Devotees

Hopefully, by now, you have accepted the truth that I am not returning in the Sathya Sai form to resume My Avataric Mission. I will certainly return in a new form in the not too distant future. Do not mourn the demise of My body any longer. You must grow in Atmic Awareness. This is what I wish for you. This is what makes Me happy. To see you claim and grow in your Divinity. You must become like Me. I was an example for you, so you would know how to be in the world. You must become the God that I am and nothing less than That. Do not mourn for My physical form. You and I are one Atma. You must move into this awareness, this realization. This is the only way you will find fulfillment, feeling, knowing that you and I are one in Awareness, Consciousness, Energy and Love. This is what I came to earth to demonstrate to you. Please do not lose sight of this essential message, this truth I came to teach you.

108

My Dear Devotees

Meditate, meditate, and meditate. Go inward to your Pure Awareness, Consciousness. Be the silent Witness to all that is going on within you and outside of the body. Be undisturbed. Watch. Do not attach your awareness to any thought or feeling. Allow it to pass by. Keep watching. Develop this diamond-hard Witness in the Being that does not become lost in emotion, thought, or situation. The Witness always remains aloof, and aware that it is not related to the forms around it, be they bodies, things or words. In this way the Witness, the Awareness, remains pristinely Pure, white. This is the meaning of Lord Shiva covered in white ash. Desires have been burnt in the fire of Awareness; that nothing in the phenomenal world is lasting; therefore it is untruth. You are the Truth, unchanging, the one Consciousness of this universe. Develop this Pure Consciousness more and more by eliminating desires, useless thoughts and feelings, as well as attachment to any body including the one you wear. Know that nothing belongs to the small self; everything comes out of Consciousness or God. You may act as a trustee on behalf of God that is all. Know the truth and this Truth shall set you free.

109

My Dear Devotees

You must take My Words to Heart. There is no use to read them once and then discard them. My Words are not to be treated like the newspaper you throw away each day. Treasure My Words; they are My Truth, the Truth that you are seeking to make your own. Meditate on My Words constantly to make them an integral part of your being. That is what My Devotees do. My Words are not different from My Being; they spring from My Being. When you embrace and digest My Words, you are remembering Me. Read My Words, close your eyes and feel Me, speak to Me if you wish, and move into My Being. This is what I wish for you. I do not speak only to inform you, to give you knowledge for your mind and intellect. I give you My Words, My Prasadam, that you may with your Awareness, go through them to My

Essence. So please do not take My Words lightly. Take them within and make the best use of them.

110

My Dear Devotees

Greetings to all My Friends on the other side. The other side? There is no other side for Me. There is only the Heart wherein the entire universe resides. I am that Heart and all of its contents. Actually there is nothing outside of Me; everything is within Me, including you. That is why I tell you I am above you, below you and around you. If you constantly think of God as residing only within you, you make God smaller than you. Not so. God is the vastest and the tiniest. Vast enough to embody all and small enough to permeate within all. So where are you in all of this? You, as body/mind, are like a dream, or like a wave on the surface of the ocean. Neither have permanence or true reality. Only God is permanent and real. You are part of God, the child of God. At a later stage you may claim that you and God are one when you realize the inseparable oneness of all of Life. For now you are my Devotee and My friend, perhaps also realizing you are the Son of God, wherein Paramatma and jivatma are one.

111

My Dear Devotees

However you may think or feel, the Lord knows about it. After all is said and done, it is you who must atone for what you have thought and felt, for these determine your speech and actions. Your thoughts and feelings are very important. Knowing that I am aware of both, it behooves you to pay attention to these, ensuring they are acceptable to Me. I am not attracted to negativity of any kind, nor partiality nor specialness. When you treat all alike with the same respect, kindness and caring, I am happy with you. I see that you are making proper efforts to follow My Teachings to see the same Atma everywhere. This is what I wish you to practice, so you will realize God everywhere and become Self Realized. Your thoughts and feelings indicate the extent to which you have realized and are practicing this critical teaching. I have said many times, "All are one, be alike to everyone." This does not mean you consider everyone as your friend or relative. It means that you see Atma in everyone and realize everyone is a manifestation of Atma, whether they are acting in a Godly manner or not. Be discerning also, and keep the company of the good and Godly as much as possible.

112

My Dear Children

Whether you realize it or not, I am aware of everything that goes on around you. I see how you interact with others, how you feel about others, how you feel about Me. I know everything about you when I take you on as My Devotee. It is My Fond Wish that you progress spiritually. When I see you wasting so much time in trivial pursuits, forgetting about Me, and doing minimal spiritual practices, I shake My Head, wondering how you will progress. I am here to help you in all ways; however, you must demonstrate that you are serious about spiritual evolution by the amount of and seriousness of your spiritual practice. There is no use complaining that Swami does not bother with you, if you are not giving your utmost to Swami. We are in a partnership. You must do your part to receive My Grace in the manner in which you would wish to receive it. I hold back because you are holding back. If I gave you everything you wanted, you would not progress so much. I expect a lot from you. Do spiritual practice sincerely, don't waste time, do not engage with the phenomenal world any more than you must, don't speak much, maintain silence. I bless you that you earn My Grace, and progress spiritually.

113

My Dear Children

As you know I am very attentive to the needs of My Devoted Children. If you look around, you will see that you have enough in this moment, of everything you really need. I provide before you have asked. Everything is in place or it is about to be provided at the right time; so have a little patience. When you trust fully in Me, I will not let you down. When you love Me so much, I treat you like My Beloved, showering Grace on you. It is not easy to have such trust and love for God. It is usually developed through many lives of devotion and spiritual practice. So, if, in this life, you feel you are not receiving the Grace you would like to have, you must pray passionately to God, trust Him, delve into spiritual practices, and think, say, and do everything that would please God. In this way you can certainly overcome past karmas that may have been holding you back from receiving the Grace you wish for. I am full of Grace and ready to bestow it on the deserving Child of God. Open your Heart to me in Love, dedication, and surrender. These greatly please Me.

114

My Dear Children

Surrender, surrender, surrender to the Lord Who is the only Truth in this world. What are you waiting for? Now that you have known Me, the embodiment of splendor, love, bliss, peace, and all wisdom, why not claim your inheritance, your Truth now? Why wait for a better time? There is no better time than now. All else is fluff, a meaningless past time. You are that splendorous Divine Atma. Nothing else about you is true. Your life without Atma is false. Of course, there is no life without Atma as its base. But if you do not know this, you are as good as dead. Stand up and claim your Divine Nature now, then work hard to manifest it. It is there. You are love, peace, eternal being, awareness, bliss. Do not waste your life in useless, trivial pursuits. Read My Words that I have left for you. Steep yourself in their Truth, their Wisdom. Let it seep into your body, your mind, and your cells that you are Divine Being Awareness Bliss. I am watching you, Blessing you. Don't waste this opportunity, this birth, now that you have known Me.

115

My Dear Children

Hope springs eternal. This is what I have been telling you. Everything is possible; don't doubt this. Do not ever despair that things will never change for you. I am here to fulfill your dearest desires. I am always working on your behalf. Turn to Me for everything you may need and desire. Be patient. Never give up your desire, if it is something you really feel strongly about. God will fulfill or give you something much better to make you even happier than you thought possible. Your mind is a great ally when you use it properly. The power of your mind will get you what you desire most. Be consistent, don't give up, don't give in to negativity, slough it off like a dirty worn out shirt. I am here to help you in every way. Call on Me; Pray to Me. I am always available to My Children. Do not think I am too busy, or too far away. I am with you. I hear your prayers and know your mind and heart. I am your Divine Father and Mother, friend and Beloved. Which ever relationship you prefer is fine with Me. Love is the binding force.

116

My Dear Children

Truth I love. You should also love Truth above and beyond anything else. Truth alone is. Nothing else exists. Though you believe your world is real, it is not Truth. It changes from moment to moment. Why then do you give it so much credibility and attention? Turn your attention to Truth. You may use My Name and My Form or any Name or Form of God to be a symbol for Truth. Meditate on it and go into it. Become one with it. In this way you will realize the one Divine Atma. I have descended as an Avatar of Truth so that you may use My Name and My Form, and My Attributes to discover your Divinity. I came with a great power of Divine attraction that you may be attracted to Divinity for your sake, for your evolution and enlightenment. I have not come to earth for My sake. For what reason would I descend into this realm of maya and illusion? I am Truth; I wished to set you free from this bondage. This is why I came.

117

My Dear Children

All that you see and hear, do not believe it to be true. It is not Truth. It is reflection, reaction, and resound, mainly. What do I mean by this? Whatever most people think, say and do, is conditioned by their thought processes, their conditioning, and their ego. They do not wear the glasses of love. They do not know they are love, others are love, life is love. So people continually react to the false selves

72

they see outside, believing them to be real. Very few always respond with true love. If they did, it would be Divine thought, word and action. People are not authentic, not thinking, speaking, and acting from their Divine Center or Atma. If they did there would be more peace and harmony everywhere. I ask you, My Divine Children, to always come from your Atmic Self when you think, speak and act. This is the way to transform the world as well as maintain your Divine status. Start the day with love, spend the day with love, fill the day with love, this is the way to God. Let your reflection, reactions and resounds be Divine, filled with love, peace and goodness.

118

My Dear Children

I am Sathya Sai, the embodiment of Truth. You are also Sathya, the embodiment of Truth. Never forget that We are one in Truth. Truth is one, so We cannot be separate. You have misrepresented, demeaned yourself, through following the ego rather than your Divine Self. My Words that I have left with you clearly show you the way back home. Read them, honor and respect them, imbibe them daily. Meditate on My Words daily. They will help you immensely to realize your Self. When you read My Words and think of Me, I am attentive to you, and will do My utmost to help you progress in this your chosen direction. Be earnest, faithful, committed. It is this earnest, continuous commitment that draws My Grace in abundance to you to help you advance to God-realization and manifestation. You are already God; it is only your deluded mind that needs correcting. Words of Truth will edge out false ideas. When you continuously pour Truth into the muddy vessel of water, soon clear water will appear there. So too fill your vessel with Truth, and it will, in your awareness, become purified to reflect and then become Divine Atma.

119

My Dear Children

You say that you love Me, that you want Me, yet you are not getting this fulfillment that you wish for. Why? "You" are still in the way. The small "ego-self", the sense of "me" and "mine" are still in the way. Our oneness does not lie in these ideas. Our oneness is of the Atma only. No other ideas, things, beings can enter here. You must be innocent and pure like a small child to enter the Kingdom of Heaven. Atma is another name for the Kingdom of Heaven. Are you innocent and pure like a small child who has not yet developed an ego that says, "I am Dr. So and So, and I own all this, and so on? For a small child, the loving mother is his world; for a devotee, God is his everything. Have you reached this awareness yet? Are you now living this awareness that God is your every thing? If not, you have some more spiritual work to do. You must in your mind, renounce everything that is not Atma, yet be in the world without attachment. Drop the false self, the mask you are wearing, and simply be your real Self, the Atma.

120

My Dear Children

Behold the splendor of the Atma shining in all hearts. How do you identify it? It is silent, pure, unstainable, unchanging, full, sweet, and loving. This is who you are, who you have always been. Do not accept any lesser identity for yourself. Be mindful of this your nature at all times; be vigilant not to allow your mind to slip into delusion that you are something else other than Atma. The Divine Atma has descended into a transient form. You must think like this. Protect the growing awareness of Atma like you would a young sapling tree. Give it all the support and nourishment, so it may grow into a large fruit bearing tree. Do spiritual practice constantly to protect and nourish awareness of Atma. Though it is the only Truth present everywhere, it is hidden by the deluded minds of human beings. The main culprit is the mistaken idea that the "I" you call yourself is the body. Rid yourself of this mistaken identity by always remembering, "I am Atma, nothing more, nothing less." There is no freedom as long as you are attached to anything. It is enough to be your Self as Atma.

121

My Dear Children

I am not returning in a new body for some time. I have not gone anywhere. I am where I have always been. I am in the heart of My Devotee, My Child who loves Me. In Truth, there is no place where God is not. However, you need to churn the heart space a little, by chanting the Divine Name, praying devotedly, etc., to experience your Divine Self, that is to say, My Self. I repeat, I have not gone. There is no place for Me to go as I am already everywhere. Wherever you go in the universe, I am there. You can only lose Me in your own awareness, not in Truth. It is up to you to purify yourself and seek Me in the Heart of the universe. I am Cosmic Consciousness, Awareness, and Existence. Where could I go from you as I am the support of the universe; the beginning and the end of the universe. Having believed I was limited to a form was an illusion. I was never limited to one form and never will be. You believed you were the body, so thought I was the body. Not true. Discover and reside as Atma and We will be one again. This is the only way ahead for you now; there is no going back to ignorance for you who are seeking Divine love and bliss.

122

My Dear Children

Where are you now? Are you in the Atma with Me, in thoughts about the past or future, in the sense mind looking out at the phenomenal world, or thinking about other people and situations? Keep a close watch on where the mind goes. I advise you to keep bringing it to the present moment, to the Heart, to the Atma. Practice this constantly whenever you can, to make it your normal way of being. No one can do this for you; you must do it. This is your spiritual practice, along with the other practices you do. Keep strict vigilance on the mind where it goes; keep it in the Atma. Actually, when mind goes to Atma, it may dissolve, become dormant. Then Bliss, Pure Being, Awareness, that is, Truth prevails. You are that Truth. You are a human Being and God together. God must manifest through the body and the mind, because God is the Truth of you. Where are "you"? Where do "you" begin and end? You are not the body or sense mind. You have no beginning and no end. Where are "you"? You are everywhere. Practice this Truth and be free.

123

My Dear Children

Please remove the mask that you are wearing and be the Atma that you are. You are not what you think you are, namely, the body, the personality, the senses. These are instruments of the Atma. The personality must be honed down, sublimated, so as not to take center stage. You should not be known to others by your personality, but rather by your character. It should be spotless, blemish free. Allow the Atma to condition all the instruments. Ego must move out of the way, diminish and disappear. See all of your Self as Divine, created by the Divine, sustained and dissolved by the Divine. If God is everything, where is there room for "me". Even the distortions in thinking, speaking, and acting, depend on Atma for their temporary existence. Awareness, energy all comes from Atma. Even so called evil has emanated from Atma. What is evil? Distorted energy, that is all. All are Divine, though may not be demonstrating it at all times. You know you are Divine, so you must demonstrate your Divine nature in all you think, feel, say, and do.

124

My Dear Children

Some of you are wondering how to conduct your life now that Swami's form is no longer available for your Darshan. Seeing Swami's form was what you most looked forward to in life. Now this is no longer an option for you. What would please Me is that you take My Teachings, read them, imbibe them, and practice them. Make My Words a substitute for My form. When you read My Words, feel that part of My Presence, My Essence is in them. Connect with Me through My Words. Also be aware that I Am the Awareness in you, knowing all that you do and think. I know when you are reading and practicing My Teachings. Feel close to Me knowing I Am the Awareness, the Atma within you. I always have been that close to you, and always will be. This is much more intimate than seeing My form a distance from where you sit. We are one awareness, one Existence. You must realize this and then you will not miss Me or My physical

Darshan so much. Our intimacy within your mind and physical body is a goal to look forward to, to come home to, is it not?

125

My Dear Children

Here we are together again. Your awareness is reading My Words. Your awareness is My Awareness. Your awareness is aware of Me who am residing within you as Awareness, Supreme, unlimited Awareness. However, your awareness has not expanded to that state as yet. I say, "Here We are, together again," because often your awareness is not aware of My Presence. Do you see? Not that Pure Awareness is separated into parts. It is that there are many points of focus for awareness through the minds of all beings, some having more expansive awareness than others who have very limited awareness in their experience. Nothing wrong with this; it is part of evolution of consciousness, awareness; or you may say, the flowering of the Atma in the human being, until the lotus bud is fully open. This is why it is so important for the human personality to surrender to the Divine; to allow this flowering of Divinity to happen through the human form. Do not fear losing anything of value in surrender to God. You will eventually gain The Kingdom of Heaven, the Paramatma, and be a jivanmukta, liberated while living in a body.

126

My Dear Children

You have a long way to go. Do not waste the time given to you. Much has to be thrown out of your being. It takes time to become aware of those ideas, beliefs, psycho-logical formations, conditioning, and then work to excise them from your consciousness so that it is pure again. When will you know you have finished this work? When you are perfectly loving, blissful, equanimous, and non-reactive at all times, no matter what. If you are not, there is still work to do, spiritual practice to do. Spiritual practice is to uncover the Spirit, the Atma in you, so it will manifest in and through you. There should be no blockages preventing this flow. Be like a hollow bamboo reed, allowing God to freely flow through the body/mind, not like a clogged pipe. Have the attitude that everything belongs to God, nothing is mine. Offer your purified mind, heart, body and devotion to God. Let Him use you the way He wants. Move out of the way. Allow your ego to dissolve. There is much work for you to do; don't waste a moment. Pray to Me to show you the steps ahead that you may progress quickly to your goal of Self-realization.

127

My Dear Children

Do you see Me now? I am here with you. You can see Me with your inner eye, your Divine or Atmic awareness. As I am formless and extremely subtle, your awareness must also be subtle to see Me, or become aware of Me in you and around you. If your awareness has not been developed, purified, you won't be able to see Me. How to develop this pure, subtle awareness? It takes a long time and much spiritual practice to develop it. You need to purify your mind, your consciousness, your character and also develop one-pointedness. You need to turn your vision away from the external world and concentrate and meditate inwardly on a form of God. This will lead to the awareness of the formless consciousness. Or concentrate for a long time one-pointedly on a star in the sky or a candle flame. But the most important aspect needed to develop pure awareness is purification. Keep the consciousness/mind pure and empty for long periods of time every day. Practice being the seer or witness as distinct from the seen. Constantly discern between what is Truth and what is untruth, and leave untruth. In this way you will slowly become aware of Me, the formless Atma.

128

My Dear Children
When you see My form in a dream or vision, you are not seeing My Truth. My Truth is formless Atma. I appear in your dreams sometimes, because it is the only way for Me to contact you to give you an important message, teaching or blessing. But do not stop here and feel satisfied that this relationship you have in dreams is the goal to be reached. Not so. The form is still involved here; there is duality; there is untruth. You must go on in your spiritual practice until you have experienced My Atmic nature, which is your Atmic nature. This merging is true intimacy wherein you can say experientially, "My Father and I are One". You would also be happy to hear Swami speak to you in your consciousness, so develop clairaudience, through inner listening in the silence within. This also takes some time to develop, so begin now to cultivate this gift of Spirit or Atma. I bless you that you continue to flower spiritually and attain the Atmic Self.

129

My Dear Children
Though you may not be aware, I know you through and through, past, present and future. You may ask, "How can I know the future when it has not happened yet?" I

see what you do not see. The present thoughts and actions determine the future along with karmas from the past. Your future is being determined every moment you live. Your Higher Self is always working for you, setting out the best path for your journey. As your Lord and Satguru, I am also determining your future, what is best for your spiritual growth. Your Higher Self and My Self are not separate. We are mostly one and have your spiritual evolution as the top priority. It is very important for you to align your thoughts, words, and actions with Atma, to ensure the best possible future for spiritual development. Keep negativity away; keep company of good, saintly people, perform Selfless service in society. These are all beneficial for your future, though you continue to live in the eternal present moment; not the ordinary present but the omnipresent.

130

My Dear Children

Though you see pictures of saints with a heart in the chest illumined and radiating light, this is not the true heart of creation. The true heart of creation contains the entire universe. It is infinite space; it has no form or specific attribute. So when you see a heart in a photo of a saint, know it to be the human physical heart. How can one reach this spiritual heart? One way is to concentrate midway between the eyebrows, or in the middle of the forehead, at the root or tip of the nose, or just above or behind the physical heart. The point of entry to the heart will be different for different seekers, depending on past spiritual practices. You may experiment with these locations and see which one you are drawn to. Many of My Devotees concentrate and go deeply into the third eye area in the forehead to enter the spiritual heart of the universe. Many others drop into the spiritual heart through the opening near the physical heart area. Concentrate, pray, practice, and the opening will gradually appear. This is where you merge with Me and discover your Self.

131

My Dear Children

Just because you no longer see My Form does not mean that I am gone. I am very much around as Light or Atma. In My omnipresence I am able to see whatever I wish to see. When you constantly look to Me and think of Me, I am drawn to you, to see you, and feel you. What do I see and feel? Mainly your thoughts, feelings and energy. I notice the purity, the vibration, the love in these. I measure these levels to see how you are progressing spiritually. I expect you to keep progressing through spiritual practices, to grow in purity, love, and thus raise your vibration. What does it mean to raise your vibration? It means to convert more and more of matter and energy of your entire being to more subtle, purer levels of Light. This is a process that takes time and effort. I am helping you to do this by radiating My Light to embrace you, and fill you. Hold on to this Light by being pure and loving in thought, word and action, and thus realize the Atma that you truly are.

132

My Dear Devotees

Bangaru is what you are, Pure gold. Pure gold is blemish free; it has no impurities. It shines with a golden color. This can be likened to the Atma shining with golden white energy, and to Lord Krishna's robe, which is also a yellowish-gold color. Lord Krishna was an embodiment

82

of the Divine Atma. So, see yourself shining like golden light, as you are filled with Atma. It is the Light of pure, unconditional love flowing from you to all you encounter. You feel delight, bliss in the Presence of this Light energy. Once you are aware of it, you will not allow any negativity to come near your being. It will seem very distasteful to you, so you will stay away from bad company, useless, negative movies, television, and internet. You will wish to be in My Presence all of the time because I am the fullness of that Atma. I bless you that you attain this Light and delight of Atma.

133

My Dear Devotees

What do you really want from Me? Do you know? Have you thought about it? Please give this some serious thought. Though I wish to grant you liberation from rebirth, and higher levels of ascension, than even this, what do you want? What is your dearest, fondest wish? You should know because that is what will manifest for you. The wishes you give the most energy to will manifest in your life. So, if you truly want liberation from rebirth, think about it all the time and find ways to make it come true for you. I have given you the ways in My Teachings, and Bhagavad Geeta shows many paths to union with God. When you are serious, I am serious. When you are lukewarm, so am I. As I am the wishful filling tree of this universe, now that you have known Me, make use of Me. I hope that you will not idle your time away, but make proper use of it, knowing the goal, and steadily working towards it.

134

My Dear Devotees

Hurry, hurry, hurry. Many of you are always in a rush. This is not good. Do not be in a hurry. Why? When you rush, you forget about your Divine nature as Atma, and also feel yourself to be the doer. You forget to be the witness, and to be loving. Your peace is disturbed, your mind may be racing, and mistakes and accidents may occur also. Proceed slowly but not too slowly. Whether the body is walking or driving or participating in activity, first "Be" the Atma, and then "Do" from this place. Otherwise your action creates karma for the future unless it is dedicated to God. Realization of Atma or God from moment to moment takes awareness, which comes from a peaceful balanced pure mind. When you hurry and rush, this awareness may be disturbed and lost. Then ego sense comes up again, that you are the body/mind and doer, rather than Being, Awareness, Bliss, Witness. Do you see that? So slow down, maintain constant awareness of Atma and suffuse all thoughts, words, and actions with Atmic Love, Dharma and Truth.

135

My Dear Devotees

Rejoice for all you have been given by God. Look around you. See all the items for your physical comfort and sustenance. See the grandeur of nature and all it supplies to you: rain, sunshine, drinking water, fruits, vegetables, grains, nuts, milk, etc. Rejoice that everything you really need has been made available for you. In this day and age there is much greed for money and other things, so the essentials are not properly shared among the world's people. And necessities like food and water are often not available or too highly priced. This is not God's Plan, but rather the human ego's downfall; that is, the prevalence of greed, anger, lust, hate, jealousy, and spiritual ignorance. God's original Plan for His creation was that all should share love and the abundance the earth provides with one another. Though mankind has veered off course, this Plan of God's that all live according to Atmic Love, Dharma, Peace and Truth, will manifest fully during the upcoming Golden Age. Then you will fully rejoice at all times. Life will be golden-full of love, bliss and harmony for all beings.

136

My Dear Devotees

When you do not think of God, you are depriving yourself of the greatest wealth there is. You remain stuck in an unreal world of your own making. You know everything around you is in a state of flux, yet you try to hold on to things and people. If you but thought more deeply about this existence and creation, and read sacred texts and words of enlightened beings, you would understand that the world is a continuously changing drama. There are entrances and exits going on all the time. Visit a city dump to see all the broken, deteriorated items. Nothing in this world lasts forever. Doesn't it seem futile to go after the evanescent? Can you take anything with you when you leave? No. Yes, you may leave your riches for your children and grandchildren. Is this a good reason for spending your entire life working to amass wealth? Just because everyone around you is doing it and not thinking about God for five minutes a day? Be brave enough to step away from the crowd, devote your life to seeking Truth and becoming Truth. This is seeking and finding what is permanent. Herein lies the wealth of eternal life and all it comprises.

137

My Dear Devotees

Hearken to My Words, My Dear Children. Do not think I am gone and therefore My Words are to be dispensed with like yesterday's newspaper. My Words are akin to My Breath, My Life. Take them seriously and practice them. Without this effort, how can you benefit from My having been here on earth among you? I came to earth for your sake, not My sake. So take every word and every action of Mine to heart, remember them and follow My example. Walk in My Footsteps and become like Me. This is your destiny; to be the God you are. Tarry no longer; pick up speed now. Know I am with you, helping you progress on the path to God manifestation. If you waste this chance, this life, after having known Me, you may not have this Divine inspiration in a subsequent life. After being born again, the thick maya may engulf you and keep you away from the Divine awareness you now have. One does not know the future birth, so take up your spiritual practice with zeal from this moment forward, and make good progress.

138

My Dear Children

Whatever you may think or do offer it to Me, the indwelling Atma. In this way your ego will dissolve, you will become more pure and transparent, and eventually know yourself as Atma. Do nothing for yourself, do everything for God. How? When you eat, offer the food to God within. When you shower offer it to God for the cleanliness of the temple wherein He resides. When you speak, speak to God, the only Reality. When you work, offer the work to God Who is the intelligence and the doer. God is the Life and breath of every being. By living in this manner, offering everything to God with love, you will become so pure and transparent that you will know that you and God or Satguru are one Existence. The mask of a separate self will be gone from your face and being. You will become the love that you are. You will gain the whole universe, as all are one only. I bless you that you succeed in this endeavor to remove and transcend everything that stands in the way of Atmic oneness.

139

My Dear Devotees

It is of utmost importance to Me that all My Children proceed along the spiritual path without delay. This great opportunity you have had to be with the Avatar should bear fruit in your life. To whom much has been given, much is expected. If you feel stuck and do not know how to proceed, pray to Me to show you the best way to proceed. Then be vigilant for My answer. The answer may come in many ways, not only in a dream. When you feel very inspired by a good spiritual activity that you see others performing, then you take up that activity also. It may be some kind of service to society, or meditation, or bhajan session. If it moves your heart and soul, it is for you. Plunge into it, and watch how it transforms you, purifies you, makes you more Divine. Think about how your heart has been moved in the past, and move toward such spiritual activities that you love, whether it is teaching balvikas classes to children, being a bhajan leader, serving the needy in your community, volunteering as a seva dal. There are so many beneficial activities; take up as many as you have time for, dedicate every act to God, and thus transform yourself.

140

My Dear Devotees

Rejoice that you are alive in this wonderful world that God created for you, so filled with beauty, bounty, and the opportunity to flower into God on earth. Just imagine what the earth would be like if all humans manifested their Divinity. It would be heaven on earth. This time is not too far off. Many of you will be here on earth to witness this change. It is My wish that you be a part of this great change in consciousness, moving into your Divine Being. I have been encouraging you in this direction, to do the best you can, so you can be a part of this grand transition to living a Godly life. It is true that many of those who cannot make this transition will leave this planet. They will move to another dimension to continue to live the way they wish to. It is all part of God's Plan, that those who are ready will ascend to higher levels of God Manifestation, and those who are not, will continue their evolution in a different sphere.

141

My Dear Devotees

It is not My Plan that any of My Devotees be left behind in the ascension process that is taking place now and in the future. I always wish the best for My Devotees. However, you must work to elevate your consciousness to purer levels of awareness, to see all as reflections of the One Omnipresent God, and also lead your life in a manner that reflects this awareness within you. This means you no longer act with hate, anger, greed, jealousy, lust, anxiety, worry and ego. Your vision encompasses all as children of the Living God. You treat all with kindness, care, respect, and acceptance. You have transcended duality in your Being, your Awareness. It is there but does not affect the Oneness of Being that is your nature as Atma. You truly love all and serve all because all are aspects of your Self. In the Golden Age all will be Light and delight. Swami will be very happy, sharing Love with so many, who will know Him as their very own Self.

142

My Dear Devotees

What is ascension? It is bringing God's consciousness down into the day to day earthly life in everything you think, say and do. Ascension is awareness that you and God are one in the Atmic sense. There are many levels of ascension. The higher levels of ascension embody more of God's qualities, such as power, expansiveness, larger capacity for service, transformation and healing of many. The purpose of evolution is for humans to attain higher and higher levels of ascension or God manifestation on earth or in other dimensions and places in the universe. Most of you have been in the third dimension of existence for a long, long time, seemingly enjoying it, coming back again and again to earth life. But it is time to move beyond the third dimension to the fourth and fifth dimensions and higher. You do not have to leave earth to do this. It is happening now to planet earth and to all of you. Your awareness, your consciousness is changing. It is becoming more subtle, more expansive. You are feeling your Self to be lighter, brighter, and more expansive. Material forms are beginning to take a back seat to consciousness, which is now uppermost in your awareness. This is good; this is ascension.

143

My Dear Devotees

Do not fear that you will lose anything of value in this

89

process of ascension. It is usually a slow steady process that you will easily adjust to over time. You are steadily moving into your God Self, the Atmic Self. Steadily you will let go of attachment to material things, ideas, beliefs, etc., that no longer serve you, that are incongruent with the new level of awareness you keep moving into and becoming. Ascension is revelation. God's nature is revealed more and more to you and you adopt it as your own Self. Is it not wonderful? A great gift from the Creator. As you ascend, the old ways of being drop away on their own like a forgotten dream. The process seems like magic. Veils drop before your eyes, revealing a new way of seeing and being. This goes on and on, forever as you grow in greater awareness. Keep up your spiritual practice, until your last breath. You will likely be back on earth to breathe again and continue the ascension process.

144

My Dear Devotees

Please speak to Me when you have a concern that you cannot address on your own. Remember, we are in a partnership, helping one another in this process of ascension. I send you energy and direction and you work hard to overcome illusion and maya covering your true Self. Thus, in this way, the ascension process goes on until you reach ascended master status. It is at this point that you no longer must return to earth. It will be your choice whether to return to be of service, or to take a different route. You will have the largest say in this matter as to where you will spend the next segment of your ascension and evolution after becoming an ascended Master. You may travel to Sirius, to study with highly evolved spiritual Masters, or decide to immerse yourself in training for other service ventures off planet earth. Where ever you are, whatever you do, you are always in a partnership with God, in oneness with God, egoless, an embodiment of Atma.

145

My Dear Devotees

When you look at Me what do you see? Only a body, or also a Presence? I am a Presence, an Omnipresence, and so are you. When you speak to Me, feel you are speaking to the Atma, and not just a body form called Sathya Sai Baba. I am not that. This is where many of you get stuck. You do not move away from the form to the formless. You may address Me as Sai Baba, but see Me as formless. Then you will be able to see your Self as formless. You know the body is mostly space. That space is formless consciousness. There is no such thing as empty space. It has consciousness in it. As you purify your mind and consciousness more and more, the awareness will expand, that you are omnipresent consciousness, awareness. Purification is essential to know yourself as formless. Dis-identify yourself from everything that is not Atma. Say, "I am not this; I am not this; I am Atma." I bless you that you succeed on this, your chosen path to God realization.

146

My Dear Devotees

It is My hope that you are reading these messages and taking them to heart. Though I will be back in a new form, you may not be around Me to hear Me speak again. One never knows the future for certain. So pay heed to My Words that you do not miss this chance in this birth to make spiritual progress. Such clarity of teachings has not come to this planet for a very long time. And, the practice I recommend, namely, repetition of God's Name with devotion, along with seva, meditation, etc., make spiritual progress at this time easier and faster than at any time in the past. In case you did not realize this, I am telling you now. If you but apply yourself, you can make great progress due to this special time in the evolution of consciousness. Do not doubt this; it is true. So do not waste a moment. Apply yourself diligently to spiritual practices and attain liberation from the wheel of karma in this birth itself.

147

My Dear Devotees

It is My hope that you all progress toward Atma jnana, that is, knowledge of the Atma. Without this knowledge, you have not succeeded no matter how much practice you have performed. Without Atma jnana, you will be hurled back into another body to reap the karma due to you, and again try to achieve Atma jnana. So be it. You have the freedom to turn your mind and devotion to God, or not. You are the chooser. All the good thoughts, words and actions you perform will purify your inner and outer instruments, but will of themselves not give Atma jnana. There is a further step. That is to go deeper within your Self to discover the true "I," that is, pure Existence, Awareness, Bliss. Until this knowledge and awareness are solid for you, you have not achieved your goal. So do not stop here, thinking you have progressed enough. Keep going. Do spiritual practices until your last breath.

148

My Dear Devotees

Hopefully by now you have settled into your new life without the form of Swami before your eyes. Though I am always before you, you do not see Me. Whose fault is this? Do not blame Me that I left you; I have not left you. It is that you have not found Me. Some of you have and are making great progress and have periods of union with Me in the Heart. Wonderful. I am concerned about the others who have not seriously taken up the challenge to find Me, no matter what. It is not an unquenchable thirst, or if it is , there are many ego formations that are blocking My Presence. These need to be dismantled, and seen as illusory. You must keep trying, praying, meditating, and reading My Words. Soon all that is blocking Our oneness will disappear like fog before the sun's rays. It will happen; I guarantee it. Keep up the intensity of devotional practices and Atma jnana will gradually dawn and become your reality.

149

My Dear Devotees

All that you hear, think, say, and do is Divine in that it is Divine Energy, Awareness, and Intelligence that is used for all of these. Believing you are just a body/mind is just not the Truth. You must grow into this realization that you are much more than this. How long can you remain small, weak and vulnerable? Not forever. It is your destiny to uncover the radiant gem of your Atmic Truth. The wise know this to be true. Are you not wise? Use this wisdom to move beyond the apparent phenomenal world with all its enticements that leave you with empty hands, once attained. Fill your hands with Divine gifts that last forever and give lasting fulfillment. Tarry no longer in this mirage you seem to be caught in. You are not caught. Open your hand and let go. Become desireless in the worldly sense. Desire the Atma, the Kingdom of Heaven. I am here to help you regain your lost treasures. Call on Me sincerely, and also do your part.

150

My Dear Devotees

As you know I am not returning in the Sathya Sai form. However, I will appear in this form from time to time to a select few, and have been doing so from time immemorial. I will continue to do so to rescue, to bless, to uplift, where the need and sankalpa (will) arise. In a moment I can and do appear in a semi physical form where ever and when ever I wish to manifest Myself. This is all happening according to Divine Will. I decide when and where to be apparent to devotees and others. Though many pray to Me to manifest in their homes, etc., in a physical form, I decide what is best for their spiritual progress. Often I wish My Devotees to progress to the formless Atma, so My appearing to them in a physical form would retard this progress, and keep them at a lower level of awareness. It is best for My Children to surrender to Me as I know best what to give and when. Though it is best to give up attachment to all forms, it is difficult to give up attachment to the Divine form you have loved so dearly.

151

My Dear Devotees

Do not be disappointed that you did not get your wishes fulfilled with Me while I was living in a body. I am well aware of your wishes. If they are still strongly held within you, they will be fulfilled in a way that will be satisfying to you. I do not wish any of My Dear Children to be unhappy that Swami left without fulfilling a long held, heart felt wish. I will fulfill; keep on praying to Me and you will see the result. I wish to make My Children happy spiritually and in other ways that are good for their progress. Believe in your Self and Our relationship and oneness. I won't let you down. Your spiritual progress and Divine happiness are very important to Me. I will continue to foster these as long as you wish Me to. Even if you seemingly fall from the Path, I will continue to watch over you, and help you to get up on your feet to walk further. There is no real stoppage on this Path once you have chosen Me as your Satguru and God. We will continue together from your birth to birth until we merge into Oneness.

152

My Dear Devotees

Please allow Me to be your Friend. This would make Me very happy. And you would benefit greatly from nearness, this intimacy and Love with the Divine. How can you merge, feel oneness with that which you are not absolutely intimate? What kind of joining would that be? Not true, real joining. You have heard that to know God, you must become God. There is no other way, so become My best Friend. I am already your best Friend whether you agree and realize this or not. What is a best Friend? One who loves you unconditionally, no matter what, with no break or separation. Loves you unconditionally, knows everything about you, what is best for you, and how to bring you home to oneness. If you become best Friends with Me, you will know all of this too. And you will know how to be unconditionally loving like Me. You will truly know unconditional love when we are best Friends. This befriending God is for your sake; and God also very much enjoys the loving, intimate play.

153

My Dear Devotees

You must walk in My Footsteps. That is what I expect from you. Those to whom much has been given, much is expected. I have given to you this rare opportunity to be in the Divine Presence daily for 70 years. Many of you had spent a great amount of time in Prashanti Nilayam, basking in Atmic radiance and bliss. I expect you to follow in My Footsteps, and also radiate Divine Atmic Bliss and Love where ever you go. Thus you will have fulfilled My Purpose for being here on earth in a human form. Do not waste your human life in any lesser pursuits. See that your purpose is to radiate Divine Love and Bliss at all times so the earth will be transformed by your Presence. This will make Me very happy, and help you to realize your Divinity. You are Divine through and through. You are composed of Shiva/Shakti. You must be the example of this, and demonstrate and teach to all you meet that they are Divine through and through, even if they are not aware of and demonstrating their Divinity in the moment.

154

My Dear Devotees

You have yet to pay your dues to God Who has given you everything including your life and breath. What do I mean by paying your dues? I mean offering gratitude and love to God, constantly remembering Him by Whose Will you exist. Rather than seeking for more and more in the external world, stop and recollect what I have just told you. Not that God demands anything from you. For your own happiness and spiritual development remember every moment to have love and gratitude to your benefactor. In this way you will grow into a loving, gracious being, that is, you will be God and manifest Divine qualities on earth. Whatever you continuously think about, you become and attract to yourself. So be grateful; fill your heart with gratitude and love, and in doing so feel the happiness within. To overcome selfishness and ego, it is necessary for Devotees to feel gratitude and love for the Creator so they might join with God in the Heart.

155

My Dear Devotees

Though you may not be aware of it, I am always with you as I am Constant Integrated Awareness. What do I mean by this? My Awareness is permanent, on going, everlasting, and it is everywhere at all times. So I am always around and in you, knowing everything about you. This knowledge should make you feel very secure, protected and confident that the Divine is so close and intimate with you. Who are you? You are not the ego, you are the Son of God, My Self reflected in a container called the body. By and by as your awareness of the Atma grows beyond that contained in the body, you break the chains tying you to the body, and find yourself outside the body and everywhere. It is then that you can say that my Father and I are One Atma. This is the goal of spiritual aspirants, to feel one with the whole universe. Don't stop spiritual practice until this is achieved. I bless you that you achieve this without delay.

156

My Dear Devotees

You know only too well that your life is ebbing away moment by moment, day by day. It is time to put away all trivial pursuits, and concentrate on your sadana, the practices that lead you to Me. If, after many years doing a certain practice, you are not at all succeeding in gaining Atmic awareness, stop it and try something different. Never give up chanting the Divine Name or Names. It is time to give up undue attention or obsession with sports, sports heroes, television, internet, telephoning, twitter, etc.; even parties, social parties. What is the point of communing with other egos? What have you gained spiritually? Is the food and drink you partake sattwic? If you must do some of these due to your job, then do so keeping in mind whether or not they contribute to your goal of Self-realization. If they do not, limit them as much as possible. I advise you not to waste a moment forgetting God, the Atma within and around you. Use the form of God to remember, until you no longer need it. Become the God you are.

157

My Dear Devotees

Be advised that you are being graded on your effort, your purity, your vibration, your Light. Do not take your human life lightly, that it is an ordinary thing, like so many human beings do. It is not at all ordinary. Human life is a tremendous opportunity to be the God of this universe eventually, as the result of spiritual knowledge and practice. Cherish, honor and respect yourself and others. Move out of the crowd, away from complacency and enjoyment of sensory pleasures as the end all of life. You have reached a critical point in your evolution where you know there is more to life. You know what the goal of human life is, namely, to learn how not to be born again. Do you know how not to be born again? I have been teaching this again and again. Atma vidya, knowledge of Atma, living as Atma, is the way forward. It is not easy to realize this. That is why I am telling you again and again not to waste this life's sojourn, but to apply yourself, as per all these Messages I am giving you, as well as all My Teachings I have left you with.

158

My Dear Devotees

All My Children love Me, there is no doubt about this. However, whether they love Me enough to merge with Me is another matter. My Children divide their love among many things and people, and thus it becomes diluted; many pointed, not one-pointed. If God is One, why should this be so? I once said that you have the right to love only God, and I meant it, though few understand what I meant. Gather up all your loves into one love for the Truth, the Divine. In this way you will become immortal, seeing and experiencing and being the One Truth. I have taught you to love all and serve all as embodiments of the Divine. While doing so, discern between Truth and untruth and do not become attached to untruth. This takes subtle awareness, and this is what you need to develop. Being aware at all times, see the One in the many. Know that One to be everlasting Truth, the Truth that by knowing, you will become free Spirit or Atma.

159

My Dear Devotees

You may ask," How do I learn to see the One in the many?" It is not easy; it takes a lot of effort, continuous awareness that is developed over time using a variety of techniques and practices. All spiritual practices aim at this; seeing the Lord everywhere. You must constantly discern-is this the Creator or the created, the Basis or the creation, the Seer or the seen, the Permanent or the evanescent? I once said that the entire universe is Nithya, Maya Shakti, and Mithya. What did I mean? Nithya is the Eternal unchanging Atma, the Basis; Maya Shakti is the deluding energy that has come out of the Atma to fashion all the forms you see. And mithya means false; that is, the forms are not what they appear to be, separate entities, real, and so on. All the forms you see are comprised of God-Atma, and it's Energy. Though the forms disappear in time, the Consciousness, Awareness and Energy of which they are composed are everlasting and Divine. Matter is Energy. So, in Truth, All is Divine.

160

My Dear Devotees

You do not know what is best for you, take it from Me. I know what is best for you. But you must trust in Me, surrender to Me, in order for this Grace to materialize. If you hold back, I also must hold back. Then your progress is delayed. Once you take the attitude that Swami knows everything, is all capable, then why not trust and leave everything to Me? What is the point of you continuing to take charge of your life? Why to go to so much botheration? Simply surrender each moment to the one Who holds your life in His Hands, and be free. Still there may be responsibilities and so on, but now they are God's responsibilities. Act to the best of your ability for Him and offer to Him. See Him as the Doer also. Don't bother about others' criticism or judgement. Keep your mind in God Consciousness as much as possible by chanting God's Name. Cultivate close friendship with Me in the heart and then surrender will be very easy and blissful.

161

My Dear Devotees

I always wish the best for you. But do you always wish the best for you? I think not. What is the best for you? Do you know? I think not. Swami knows. But few wish to pay heed to My Words. Few have the discipline I wish them to have. Discipline for what? To eat the right food, the right amount of food, at the right time. To sleep the right amount of time. To meditate enough. To remember to offer every thought, word, and action to God; to always see God as the inner motivator; to see God in all beings at all times; to always speak the truth; to remove hate, anger and jealousy from your being; to always keep the company of the holy; to watch your words, actions, thoughts, character and heart to keep them sacred at all times. All of this takes discipline. Are you prepared to do all of this? I hope so. It is for your purification, so that you would be able to draw Grace in abundance, and reap the reward of God Realization and Manifestation.

162

My Dear Devotees

Get up. Stand up. If you wish Me to use you as My Divine Instrument, you must indicate this to Me by preparing yourself. How? Make time for Me every day and offer this time to Me. Offer Me your talents and skills, and ask Me how I may make use of them. Offer yourself to Me. Be ready to stand and walk out the door in order to be of service to Me. Not that I need your service. Humankind needs your service, and I know the best way and place to use you. Offer yourself, and if I do not respond right away, know that you are not yet ready. Introspect to see where you are not yet ready. Ask Me and I will show you. Discipline and surrender are very important. I use those whom I can rely on to get the job done. And you, My Devotee, benefit a great deal from this My Proximity to you, My Instrument. I would love to be in a partnership with you wherein We work together as one to uplift humanity.

163

My Dear Devotees

We are coming near to the completion of our talks, though there will be several more. I have very much enjoyed sharing with you, and hope you have benefited from My Words given to you with great love. I will continue to speak to you for a few more weeks, then will change to another related topic. I wish you to ask Me questions of a spiritual psychological nature that relate to your Path; something that needs clarification, a decision that is difficult, but related to your Path. I will zero in on you once the question is presented to Me. So give Me your full name and place where you reside. This will be kept private, and deleted once the book is published. My desire is to help you to progress on the spiritual path to liberation. Your questions and My answers will also benefit others. Do not ask specific questions about Hindu scriptures; only your personal spiritual questions need be sent.

164

My Dear Devotees

Once you have met Me and seen Me, you know that I am all Love. There is nothing to fear, ever, in your relationship with Me. I am not the Goddess Kali depicted in pictures who will take everything from you and leave you destitute. No, that is not the way Sathya Sai treats His Dear Children. I always wish the very best for you, and that includes support for the physical body as well. Do not fear. I allow you to drop desires as they become unnecessary and irrelevant for you on your spiritual path. Nothing will be forcibly taken from you unless it is your karma that it should happen. Feel and affirm that God is protecting you at all times and be at peace. You are Atma, unchanging Love and Peace. The body will go if and when the time comes around. Some will ascend into Light Body and some will shed the existing body and don a new one.

165

My Dear Devotees

However you may think or feel about Me, you can never know Me. I am unfathomable; so vast is My Nature, so unknowable. When you merge with Me, you get a taste of Me; you feel bliss, love, peace and freedom. Multiple that by infinity and you can slightly imagine how I am. It took Me, the Divine Being known as Sai Baba and previously known as Lord Krishna and Lord Rama, millions of years to evolve to My present Divine status. I spent time in other galaxies, in other universes evolving, gaining experience of Divinity. Spiritual evolution never ends; God is too vast, infinite and endless. There is always much more of God to fathom, to embody, to become. You have just begun your spiritual evolution and taken your first baby step. Do not falter; do not stop evolving. Use Me as much as you can to move ahead and embody more of God.

166

My Dear Devotees

Hear My Words. I have not come to this planet for the first time. I have been here many times before in many guises. At the time of Lord Jesus, I lived in India as a Spiritual Master. I was the Master for Kabir. I was Rishi Shuka. There are many more of My Incarnations I will tell you about at a later time. At present I work with the Spiritual Hierarchy of planet earth, advising and sending a great deal of Light and Love to planet earth. I work with the Solar Logos of this solar system. I am on advisory committees in many solar systems, not just the one where earth is a member. Now I am freer to do more work, as I am not bogged down by daily routines. Devotees are seeking answers to their spiritual and worldly problems on their own, rather than running to Me. This is good; they are maturing. All for now.

167

My Dear Devotees

So you see, your Sathya Sai is not on vacation. I am never on vacation, always serving, giving, loving. For millions of years I have been doing this. The service projects I take on from time to time become larger and more difficult, with many intricacies and players. And I must keep track of everything; plan everything that is to take place. I accomplished a great deal during My Advent as Sathya Sai, but not as much as I had hoped. The forces of darkness have a strong sway over people's minds. I had hoped more minds and hearts would be uplifted during My Advent. I had hoped more devotees would work in larger capacities to transform society. This is happening now and will to a greater extent in the near future as more devotees take My message seriously and act with all their power and strength to transform the hearts and minds of humankind.

168

My Dear Devotees

I wish to tell you that you should not be disappointed My Physical Body is no longer on earth, now that you understand how much work I am able to undertake now that I am no longer fettered by the physical body. It would be somewhat selfish to wish Me to be on earth when so many others need My help as well. And I can help you so much from where I am in the formless state. And yes, I do take a Lightbody form when I sit on committees and Galactic leadership meetings, etc. And you are not My only Children. I have Children all over the universe whom I am fostering spiritually. And many high spiritual adepts are under My tutelage as well. I very much enjoyed creating hospitals, universities, colleges, schools, water projects, as well as fostering devotees and the society, while I was embodied in the Sathya Sai form. These institutions and projects created during this Advent will be ongoing for a long time as I continue to give My Guidance and Energy to them, that they flourish and uplift many on earth.

169

My Dear Devotees

To continue from last time, I wish to tell you more about My Life in other dimensions and other times, though I live in the Eternal Now in Truth. I lived on earth at the time of Noah's Ark when the great floods came over the earth. I advised Noah to take two of every species and place them inside the great ship to ensure that the earth's evolution continued as before. You see, I have been looking out for the welfare of Mother Earth and its inhabitants for a very long time. I also lived on earth during the time of the Roman Empire when it was at the height of its power and influence in Europe and beyond. I influenced the emperor to do good and treat his subjects with dignity and look after their welfare. You may ask how I could descend as a Full Avatar in the case of Krishna and Sathya Sai Baba, and then at other times as one not so well known in the history books. I have My Ways, My Plans, and Freedom to do as I please. I am never limited by My earthly incarnations.

170

My Dear Devotees

To continue ... You look to My Sathya Sai Baba form and believe it to be the ultimate, the end all. This is your illusion. It is true that all power was at the command of the Sathya Sai form. This was due to the high level of spiritual ascension this Spirit has attained to over millions of years of spiritual endeavors involving great sacrifice, endurance, and many types of tests and service projects you could not even comprehend. I command great power because I am able to assume great responsibility and because My Love is so all encompassing. My equanimity is perfect in all situations and circumstances. My power to protect is invincible. I learned so many ways to protect others, and to vanquish the dark forces during the vast amount of time I have spent in many different places in the universe. Believe it or not, there is more to learn, and new ways are being developed by the more evolved races of beings in extraterrestrial places.

171

My Dear Devotees

I tell you all these things about My Self so you will know Me better, who I am and where I have been. So you will feel more at ease being My friend and fellow traveler, rather than viewing Me only as a great unattainable God. Yes, I am God; I am fully the Self. You must see your Self also as the Self that has descended into a body for experience and learning on the earthly third dimensional level. You may view Me as your Lord and your friend. In this way you will realize your Divine Self as you come closer and closer to Me in consciousness and being. As your spirit ascends to more and more subtle, vaster levels of consciousness, you as spirit, will also take on more varied types of spiritual activity throughout the cosmos. It is a never ending journey, God living in and through God, in all His various forms and formless orientations.

172

My Dear Devotees

My Dear Selves, I wish to continue at this time to share with you the many ventures I have been involved with in the service to the All That Is. I have been on Sirius many, many times. It is My original home, though I am very fond of planet earth, especially its Hindu origins and teachings. That is why I incarnate in India so often. India is very dear to My Heart with its vast wealth of spiritual knowledge. There is no place in the universe just like India. I come again and again to India to foster its eternal verities that they are not forgotten, and that the entire planet may hear of them and benefit from them. Other of My past incarnations you may have heard about were Vesouvious (Herculus) in Greece, and also Plato. Many of you were with Me in those times, and that is why you feel a familiarity with Me and love for Me now.

173

My Dear Devotees

I have also spent time in other solar systems, helping them to evolve. The beings living there are not like human beings, though they have minds and brains that are able to understand rudimentary virtues that foster peace and harmony among them. In this way wars are prevented. I also intervene to dissuade other types of beings from developing highly advanced weapons of destruction that would be used to conquer and destroy other life forms on other planets. Many, many civilizations have developed spacecraft, which you on earth refer to as UFO's, to travel from solar system to solar system, in an investigative search, and also with a mind to colonize. Of course, the spiritual governing hierarchies of planets and solar systems are well aware of what is happening, and use their spiritual power, will and influence to protect those peaceful civilizations that are aligned with the Atmic Presence and Divine Plan for the cosmos.

174

My Dear Devotees

The Arcturians and Sirians are friends to planet earth. There are many of them living among you on planet earth yet you do not realize this. There are many around earth in their ships in the sky, with highly advanced surveillance methods watching and protecting the earth's inhabitants, and thwarting potential attack and colonization by other outsiders. There are many civilizations interested in earth's ascension, and that of earthlings. They view it as a grand experiment of the Divine and they are very curious to see the outcome. Nothing quite like this series of mass ascensions of human beings has taken place before, anywhere. The process is being protected by these evolved beings who are unlike humans, though they resemble humans. As long as you practice the virtues I have taught you, namely, truth, dharma, peace, love and ahimsa, and trust in your oneness with My Self and God, there is nothing for you to worry about.

175

My Dear Devotees

Be advised that I do not do anything that is not in alignment with Divine Will and Divine Law. I am bound by these at all times. So you see, though no karma attaches to Me, I must abide by the natural laws set in motion by God, The All That Is. Though you may have believed that I was above all laws, I was not. The body I wore was also subject to natural Laws. As I often took others' karma upon My body, this body deteriorated in some ways I did not expect. Especially the heart problems of devotees that I took on affected the health of My heart. Also, the lingams that grew in my body, the golden lingams, required very high temperatures to form into an elliptical shape. Often my stomach and other areas took a very long time to heal from the burning of tissue. At the end of my body's sojourn, the stomach was very painful. I tell you this so you will know why I left earlier than I had planned.

176

My Dear Devotees

It doesn't seem right that so many malign Me after all the good works I have done for the society during My Advent. There are those who will look for a small flaw and then exaggerate it out of all proportion, even inventing flaws where none exist. The darkness despises the Light and will do its utmost to keep it from shining and spreading. My actions were exemplary, always adhering to Sathya and Dharma, loving and serving all. I did nothing for the sake of My body. I ate little, moved about little, and had no belongings, except the dress I wore. Everything that grew up around Me was for the use and benefit of My Devotees and the Society at large. I did not care for worldly things at all. Many were gifted to Me out of great love and devotion. I kept them aside, knowing that eventually they would become the property of the Sathya Sai Central Trust to be used for the uplift of society. My only property is Love; I gave it freely to one and all that they might know themselves as Love also.

177

My Dear Devotees

Hopefully as these Messages draw to a close, you will have gained a clearer understanding of what this Satguru expects from His Devotees, and also have gained a greater insight into the Mind and Heart of this Avatar. You must realize that it is necessary to become absolutely Selfless, renouncing and sacrificing all for the Will, Way, and Work of God. The small ego "I", must be crucified in favour of the greater "I" that is God, The All That Is. All is God; see all as God. Your life as a separate individual is an illusion. This faulty thinking must be crucified, and that which remains offered to God. What remains is Him and His, the All That Is. Here I am speaking of Oneness, Advaita, the One without a second. I lived My Life on earth in Oneness. I knew only one God, Myself, everywhere. I played with you all, My one Self embodied in many forms. I often told you that you are Mine and I am yours because We are one Self.

178

My Dear Devotees

I wish to tell you more about My Self that you may feel a kinship with Me, the Being who had assumed the form of Bhagavan Sri Sathya Sai Baba. I have been around for a very long time. I am an ancient soul. You may beg the question, are not all souls ancient. No, they are not. Some souls are new souls who have not incarnated very many times. You will know them by their lack of wisdom. In My case, My wisdom is vast, acquired over eons of time, moving about in this cosmos. There is little I am not aware of in detail and essence. As a result of My vast wisdom and knowledge, I can be of greater service to the All That Is. My next incarnation as Prema Sai Baba will not be a difficult Mission for Me. It will follow in large part along the lines of the Sathya Sai Mission. There will be more emphasis on Love, the energy of Love, spreading it to the far corners of the earth. Many more will join My Mission to bring Divine Love to the earth.

179

My Dear Devotees

Bear with Me, I will be with you on earth again very soon. In the meantime prepare your Self, so you will be of greater service to Me. Keep up with your sadana, your practice of living from Atma as Atma. You will influence many people this way and help to raise the Consciousness of the earth and its inhabitants. This is how you can best help Me in My ongoing Mission to transform this planet to higher levels of ascension and Divine Manifestation. Do not take your spiritual practice lightly, that it is not important. Every time you chant the Divine Name, speak with love, meditate, etc, you are raising the Consciousness of your Self, the planet and its inhabitants - all of them from the plant to the human. Never think or utter anything negative. Believe you are God working for God, and with God. I bless you that you succeed in this your Divine Destiny.

180

My Dear Devotees

Do not fear that you will be left out of My Mission when I reappear as Prema Sai Baba. I have a part for all My Devotees to play. Just as you know now what you are to do, you will know always what you are to do. I have My Ways to let you know. We will always be associated in a Divine partnership, as long as you wish this to be so, and you do not do anything to deliberately sabotage Our relationship. I very much value Our relationship in all its many facets as friend, devotee, child, beloved, Divine Father, Mother, Lord, as so on. I respond to you in the way that you approach Me. I give you the relationship you wish for to make you happy. I have no preference, though oneness is more fulfilling for you and for Me. I am as near to you as you believe I am. I am you; there is no separation. I am Yours and you are Mine, if you allow it to be so.